Get d' picture!

KEY TO EMPOWERMENT

K. DENNIS CHIEDU

Get d' picture!

Get d' picture!

Copyright © 2016 by Dennis Kenechukwu

All rights reserved.

No part of this publication may be reproduced, distributed, or transmitted in any form or by any means, including photocopying, recording, or other electronic or mechanical methods, without the prior written permission of the publisher, except in case of brief quotations embodied in critical reviews and certain other noncommercial uses permitted by copyright law.
For permission requests, write to the publisher, addressed, "Attention: Permissions Coordinator," at the following address.
Keli and Josh Ventures, PO Box 770023, Houston TX 77215, or contact by email at kandjventures04@gmail.com

Unless otherwise indicated, all Scripture quotations are taken from the King James Version of the Holy Bible.

Scriptural quotations marked NLT (New Living Translation) – Online edition, by Tyndale House Publishers Inc. © 2016; NIV (New International Version), Online edition, © 2011-2016 Biblica.

ISBN 13: 978-0-9976628-0-1

Printed in the United States of America. All rights reserved under International Copyright Law. Contents and/or cover may not be replicated in part or in whole in any form without the express written approval of the publisher

K. Dennis Chiedu

Get d' picture!

K. Dennis Chiedu

"... and with all thy getting, get understanding."
Proverbs 4:7 (KJV)

Get d' picture!

TABLE OF CONTENTS

Table of Contents	…………………	6
Acknowledgements	…………………	7
Introduction	….…………………..	9
Foreword	………………………	15
Chapter I:	Where we need Understanding	18
Chapter II:	How to get Understanding	34
Chapter III:	Where we gain Understanding	40
Chapter IV:	Benefits of having Good Understanding	51
Chapter V:	Discovering You	59
Chapter VI:	Discovering Your Purpose	81
Chapter VII:	Safety Ships	95
Chapter VIII:	People that had a glimpse of Who They were	104
	Conclusion:	116

ACKNOWLEDGEMENTS

Numerous people motivated me in one way or another and they are part of the reason I embarked on this journey. I salute every one of you out there who contributed positively or negatively and through whom I was moved to write this book. May the Almighty God bless you exceedingly.

I want to thank everyone who stood with me during this writing process – my family and friends. Your support and encouragement were priceless. The understanding shown and the sacrifices made at this time were very much appreciated.

I want to thank especially my late mother and friend – Mrs. Felicia Kenechukwu, for all you did for me. I will never forget your sacrifices.

I want also to thank Ms. J. Lacie Redding, who painfully read through and edited this work. You brought out the beauty of the book. May the good Lord continue to bless you to enable you to do more for Him.

My appreciation equally goes to my pastor, John Fowler, Ph.D. for writing the foreword to this book. Thanks for your kindred spirit.

Get d' picture!

My most thanks goes to the Holy Spirit that keeps inspiring me to write. I could not have done this on my own. May He alone be praised forever – Amen.

INTRODUCTION

What I discovered in the short time I have so far lived is that a lot of folks today live far below their potentials and purpose and they neither know nor realize it. They think that the level at which they currently operate is the best that life can offer them; as a result they resigned to that conviction. When you ask them if they think they could do better, you discover they have no idea.

But friend, I want to let you know this: that concept is far from the truth. That is the lie of the devil from the pit of hell to deceive and keep people down, and also keep them from vigorously pursuing and attaining their destinies. Knowledge has a way of stirring one up and that is the essence of this book – to inform and stir you up to reach your greatest potential. The information at ones disposal determines the level of knowledge they have. That also determines the directions they follow and their reach in life.

Get d' picture!

To reach your greatest potential, you need to understand who you are. You have to come to terms with your capacity: your personality, purpose, assignment, expectations and others. You have to be able to find answers to the following questions. *Who am I? What am I doing here? What can I do? Can I change a thing or make something better?*

Understanding who you are has a way of putting you fast on the highway of success. It reveals to you the actual you: what you are designed to be and to do, not what you were made to believe and think you are. When one gets the mental picture of his or her personality and hidden abilities or what he can accomplish and where he can go, the individual can no longer be restrained or stopped from becoming exactly that. He can only go forth achieving those things he sets out to accomplish, persisting.

At this time when you see the person, he will be poised to becoming all he was made to be. When you see him talk, that attitude will be in his conversations. As he walks, you see it in his strides. He radiates the confidence in whatever he does. With all due respect, our president was called naïve and he even behaved that way in his first few years in office. There were series of uproar among his opponents when he went to Saudi Arabia and Japan and bowed to the royalties. Americans were very upset. I think he was yet to understand the office, the prestige and power of the U.S. president. He was kind of taking it – this is Barack Obama from South Side Chicago, but it was far from that. However, after many years of understanding the presidency, it became a different ball game altogether. After those periods of missteps, the tide changed; come and see how he started to deal with foreign leaders, and they called at his beckon, at his will. Many even began to lobby and queue to see him, which were sometimes turned down. By this time, he had come to terms with what he is and what he represents, the power behind him and more.

This is what understanding can achieve in an individual, especially where the person has some power to flex. Some later events like his dealing with Russia after the annexation of Crimea in Ukraine showed the president had come to fully grasp the authority and power he commands. You saw how he used his presidential veto slamming sanctions at random against Russia.

There were even reported cases of his not wanting to deal with Netanyahu, the Israeli Prime Minister, during that time too, although that logjam changed overtime. That demonstrates how he came around and took control and command of the situation.

I also remember his Nigerian counterpart – Goodluck Jonathan in his early days in office. He too, with all due respect, equally acted so inexperienced when he took office. People were poking into his eyes and he did nothing. Even the world media labeled him "weak." Those days when I read the news, they said the "weak Nigerian central government," but that narrative eventually changed over time. He was later accused of series of violations from the same people who once labeled him weak. The man has come to understand and flex the power he commands and the authority behind him. Back then when you looked at him, he looked confused but when he began to exude a level of confidence, Nigerians liked it. Some wanted him to go further, especially to fight the cabals controlling the country and festering corruption in the system, and also deal decisively with the Islamic terrorists and insurgency that has put a black face on the nation, which critics say he mishandled.

Many believers, at times, find themselves in this type of quagmire, some might even be in one right as you read this book, but what gives one edge over the situation is the level of understanding the individual possesses about himself; what he represents and about the situation at hand. Some can muddle things up or make positive marks depending on the way they manage such times.

Understanding has a way of programming one's mind to come to terms with the facts, which makes the individual to stand up and look the situation in the face, as well hold their head high while producing results.

When you understand who you are, it enables you to know where you are weak and vulnerable and prepare to tackle any challenge that arises in that area. It also helps you know your strength and how to maximize and take advantage of it.

The centurion who met with Jesus in the Bible (Matthew 8:9) understood authority. If you listen to his demand from the Lord, he spoke as a man that had a full grasp of what he wanted, and the position of the person he was making the demand from. *"I am not worthy to have you under my roof. I am a man under authority, I say to one go here and he goes and the other over there and he goes. Just say the*

word and my servant would be healed." He never sounded like a man who did not know what he wanted or who he was dealing with. You remember the response he received; Jesus said He had not found such faith in Israel. Understanding gives you clarity and boldness; it also gives you courage that enhances your demeanor. You know the end result; he got what he demanded. Praise God! You can too.

Some say knowledge is power, and I believe the Lord wants us to be empowered with knowledge that will transform our lives to make it what He wants us to be. Early one morning, in late December 2012, while vacationing with my family in San Francisco, California, God dropped these words into my heart, ***"Understand who you are in the Lord."*** This was while I was having my quiet time. I began to ruminate over those words. I discovered a lot of people are suffering, I mean believers because they do not understand who they are (their position) in the Lord and that God wants a change to that. When you understand who you are in the Lord, your son-ship and the redemption package available to you, it helps you take your rightful place in life and your desires.

As long as they do not come to terms with who they are in the Lord, victory will keep eluding them. They will continue to complain and wallow in mediocrity.

In Psalm 2:7-8, the Bible says, ***"I will declare the decree: the Lord hath said unto me, Thou art my son; this day have I begotten thee. Ask of me, and I shall give thee the heathen for thine inheritance, and the uttermost parts of the earth for thy possession."***

Get d' picture!

Until one understands who he actually is and the rights and privileges available for him to enjoy in the Lord, he may not be in the position to declare or assert his or her rights over anything including God's promises, and as long as he remains in that state, the individual will continue to struggle.

However, my prayer and the essence of this book is to stir you up, that God may open your eyes as you read, to enable you to understand all He wants you to apprehend for the purpose of your becoming all you can be in life and destiny, and be a blessing to your generation in Jesus name - Amen.

K. Dennis Chiedu

10 – 19 – 15

FOREWORD

As stated in His Word, God has a plan and purpose for your life. "And we know that God causes everything to work together for the good of those who love God and are called according to His purpose for them." (Romans 8:28 NLT) God has you on this earth for a reason and He intends to solve some of the world's problems through you. It's important that you not miss His plan and purpose for your life.

This book, *Get d' picture! KEY TO EMPOWERMENT*, is birthed out of an encounter with God in December of 2012 during the author's quiet time. God dropped into his heart the words, "Understand who you are in the Lord." Meditating on these words, Dennis knew many believers are frustrated and missing God's plan and purpose until they understand who they are in Christ and discover the problems they were created to solve. God has an assignment for each of us. Let's not miss it.

Get d' picture!

Dennis Kenechukwu is an evangelist, speaker and teacher; who has helped plant churches in the Nigerian cities of Lokoja, Warri and Port Harcourt. This book is rooted in scriptures and is both testimonial and biographical as Dennis shares from his life experiences.

I encourage you to read this book with the goal of understanding who you are in Christ and God's purpose for your life. And as you read, I bless you to set your face, determined to do His will and know that you will triumph because the Sovereign Lord helps you. God intends to solve some of the world's problems through you. Trust Him and let Him use you in ways that are beyond you!

John Fowler, Ph.D.
Lead Pastor (Retired)
Christ's Church
Houston, TX

CHAPTER ONE

Where we need understanding

I will say that we need understanding in our everyday lives and activities. Whenever we need open doors and/or want to get ahead, understanding matters a lot. Whenever we want to pursue any goal or engage in a venture, understanding is vital. Understanding is key! ***No matter how strong or powerful a door is, once you get the right key, you can open that door.*** (Dennis - 2:04 a.m. – 04/26/14).

Most things in life are controlled by doors. Every door that leads to an important place in life or to where treasures are stored up usually has a lock on it. For one to have access, the individual will have to locate the right keys or codes for them to unlock and get the doors open. Until one gets the doors opened, they may never be in the position to enter and achieve what they desired.

Get d' picture!

The same thing is applicable to many life situations whether they are projects, careers, marriages, businesses, industries or discoveries, they could be in leadership, but it takes one finding the right key to enable them unlock the doors and get through to succeed in these areas; that is the reason we need understanding. Understanding is that key we need to excel in our careers, in our jobs, in our endeavors and even in marriages. No wonder hiring managers usually want to see your years of experience in a particular area or field - you are seeking employment before they hire you. They want to be sure Stella or Steve has the requisite knowledge or understanding needed for the particular field and position they are seeking. In proverbs 3:19, the Bible says that through wisdom the Lord founded the earth but through understanding He established the heavens; implying that understanding is that ingredient that helps one to establish whatever they set out to do.

The man whom Jesus referred to in the Bible (Luke 19:20-26), whose master gave a talent as he embarked on a journey; the one that buried the talent, did not understand who he was, his purpose and the trust reposed on him by his master. As a result, he did not bother to develop his talent to become what he was designed and expected to be for the benefit of his master; rather, he chose to bury it. But he lost out. He thought he was being smart. That should not be our lot. We are expected to develop ourselves and every gift the Lord has bestowed upon each one us for the benefit of the Lord and our community. The truth remains that you will be rewarded accordingly and bountifully when you do that. I have never seen anyone the Lord used and dumped or left empty handed. Look around you and see those that are using their talents to serve God, do you see any of them not blessed of the Lord? Are they barely surviving? That is a good lesson to us.

At home

We all need understanding to enable us relate effectively to every member of our family and to keep the family intact. There is no silver bullet in dealing with every member of our family because individually we are uniquely made and operate that way. Parents will have to deal with every child according to their differences. If you want to treat Bill the way you do Tom, there may be trouble. Same thing when you want to treat Agnes and Sophia same way.

This same thing is applicable to couples. Sometimes it could be costly to expect your spouse to behave like your parent or the other person. A guy may be tempted to expect his wife to treat him the way his mother would do or the wife expecting her husband to deal with issues as her father would. People are not the same and that is why we need understanding to help us handle such situations as they come. You need to take time to study the package you have on hand in your home so that you do not mishandle it. Note: that things worked in a particular way with an individual does not mean that it can work same way under same scenario with another individual. Human beings differ from each other and also are complex. That is why concerted efforts are needed to study and understand how things work with different persons in your home. Some kids are independent-minded while others like to be dependent; if you treat them the same way, you cause trouble in the home.

Also for some people that have had other relationships prior to the one they are presently in, there is usually the tendency to compare your spouse with your exes. If you find yourself doing this, you are already plotting the downfall of you current relationship. The reason is that there are no two people that are the same.

Let us also not forget the sex differences. The chemical balances and makeup of the male and female genders differ. What keeps the union or relationship going is understanding among the partners. To be clear, as long as the differences exist, there will continue to be tense times and disagreements along the line but with understanding, the friction is reduced. Someone said it is part of human nature to quarrel. You may or may not agree with that assertion but as long as humans are free-thinking beings with differing tastes and choices, you should expect it. What you need here is to be able to handle it when it eventually comes so that it does not get out of hand or blow up. Even same sexes and identical twins sometimes disagree too, showing the complexity of life.

To excel in our studies

You need this understanding to excel in your studies or when learning a vocation. When you understand yourself, you already know your capacity. With that, you plan on how to tackle and pursue your studies. Some people tend to follow others not knowing they do not have the same capacity as them, and when the chips are down, they are left behind. Those days when we were in secondary school or high school, there were sets of students that played a lot. You only see them in class but hardly see them reading regularly afterwards. They have sharp brains or are simply intelligent. We also had the not so sharp ones. In addition of not having sharp brains, they were not also smart enough to understand that. When the exams came, you saw them running helter skelter as if the exams were sudden rather than pre-planned events. At the end of the day, they failed their exams or merely passed but the other group excelled. If they had understood that they were slow learners, they would have started early to read and not follow those sharp ones that deceived them but who usually took the first positions despite not spending so much time reading.

I remember also, during my undergraduate days at the university, that I was a short time span reader. I like reading intermittently – one hour, I get up and walk around a while and sometimes chat before going back to read. Once I do this, I refresh my brain and I get hold of everything I read in the next hour. I also understood that I am easily distracted by little noise when I study. It made me choose friends who were like-minded and also best times that suited my kind of reading habit. That led me to form a reading habit that was usually late nights when other students were going back home to bed. Between 11:00 p.m. and 3:00 a.m., the classrooms were quiet. At this period, I would be out there reading. Afterwards, I would head back to the hostel to get some sleep to help rejuvenate for the business of the upcoming day.

My reading pattern also affected my eating habit. I discovered that once I ate, my body would be heavy and want to sleep. It led me to eat early in the evening before sleeping to wake up about 10:00 p.m. to get ready for my studies or not eat at all until I was done with studies.

I also knew a lot of us then who could read very well in a noisy environment. Even if the class was like a marketplace, they did not care but I dared not follow them less I would not have graduated.

This is the kind of understanding one needs to have about themselves to excel in their studies.

In our work places

Like home, one needs to understand the dynamics of human nature in order to deal effectively with colleagues at workplace. If you do not have this understanding, you may not succeed in your work environment.

Also you need the knowledge of your craft to succeed where you work. As a business-orientated environment geared towards profit making and excellence, you will have to show your expertise and professionalism as is in your craft. There are targets and deadlines to meet and you cannot afford to do otherwise. You have to also study the dynamics of your workplace in other to meet up with productions as expected.

As we transact

To successfully transact your business, you need good knowledge of your trade. People come to you because they believe you can handle their concerns. But a situation where they come they discover you do not really command the knowledge of the issue as they thought and want, then you better start closing shop.

In relationships

The Bible enjoins husbands to deal with their wives with knowledge (1 Peter 3:7). Every man that wants to live with a woman has to take time and study their wives. If you put your thinking cap as you would to fellow men or react as you would to other men when dealing with women, you will ever get it wrong. Women are very different from men and the same thing applies to the women folks too. Usually, it is easier for the women to engage in conversation, which is not typical of most men. Generally women like to talk about their issues or lash out during pains and problems, but men usually withdraw and be alone when in pain or having issues. Also some men are addicted to sport which irks their wives. These have led to a lot of serious issues that would not have been issues at all if there were gender understanding between the two. There should be a balance. That is where understanding is very, very essential. Also as we make decisions and choice of life affairs, we need understanding of issues, especially where two kinds of persons are involved.

Leadership & Decision Making

In order to be an effective leader that makes wise and right decisions, understanding is very essential. In fact, you cannot lead efficiently if you lack vital understanding needed in areas of your trade or assignment in life. Understanding is what gives you focus, direction and strength for the vision you are pursuing.

Jesus was on a mission here on Earth hundreds of years ago, but take a look at the account of the Bible as to how he succeeded in accomplishing the assignment.

"Looking unto Jesus the author and finisher of our faith; who for the joy that was set before him endured the cross, despising the shame, and is set down at the right hand of the throne of God." Hebrew 12:2 KJV

When you look at the phrase ***"… who for the joy that was set before him endured the cross…"*** it does not depict a person ignorant, who was looking to chance or luck somewhere to propel him to succeed in his assignment. No, He understood what was up against Him and decided; it was an informed choice that He made and the rest was history. As leaders, understanding your duty and roles should be a serious business. As parents, we should know our duties and responsibilities, and also perform them accordingly. So many parents have lost the respect of their children simply because they have no grasp of what parenting is all about. People think that just having a baby makes one a parent. It is far from that; parenting has greater responsibilities and parents should step up to their duties. As parents, you should know what children are like; a lot of them are selfish and demanding. They are not even caring enough to show appreciation at certain period of their lives. They will tie you down; they are great job to handle. But, they are also bundles of joy for families and a desire nearly every family is willing to have and invest in. One thing I discovered is that every good and precious thing comes with a price, children are not exempted. But when you know that such times would come, you arm yourself so as to effectively tackle them as they show up.

Also as a manger in an office or anywhere, arm yourself with the understanding that managing human beings is a tough task. Study human relations and psychology. Common sense is very important too. You also need the wisdom and grace of God here. Find out things about different types of people you meet day-by-day. People from different backgrounds behave differently. Oftentimes their backgrounds influence their sense of judgment. When you understand that humans are complex, you prepare yourself in a way that will help you manage them, as well produce needed results without undermining your position and the establishment. That was exactly what Jesus did and succeeded in His task.

Get d' picture!

If Jesus did not understand who he was and his mission while on Earth, He would have derailed when pressure mounted following the unkind treatments and rejection from the same people He came to deliver. John 1:11 (KJV) says, *"He came unto his own, and his own received him not (rejected Him)."*

But because he foreknew these things would take place, he was prepared for them. He kind of developed shock absorber and was not taken by surprise by the unfolding events as they happened. Leaders should take note here, knowing what to expect or seeking to know what to expect in a project puts you steps ahead of any eventuality. And when the unfortunate began to happen, you saw He was in total control and never threw in the towel. Even when facing death, He was still faithful to the mission. Standing alone before Pilate, He never shied away from testifying to that assignment,

"Pilate therefore said unto him, 'Art thou a king then'? Jesus answered, 'Thou sayest that I am a king. To this end was I born, and for this cause came I into the world, that I should bear witness unto the truth. Every one that is of the truth heareth my voice'." John 18:37 KJV

However, despite His control over the mission, there was a time too when emotions clashed with the realities of the mission. Such times will always show up when situations and assignments get real and tough.

"And he went a little farther, and fell on his face, and prayed, saying, O my Father, if it be possible, let this cup pass from me: nevertheless not as I will, but as thou wilt." Matthew 26:39 KJV

This passage shows Jesus displayed humanity even as He fought back to subdue the self. A time like this will usually show up in the life of every leader – pressure to throw in the towel. But focus and thorough understanding of the prevailing circumstances and the anticipated outcome is what strengthens the person and eventually brings the game changer. Whatever subsequent decisions and actions a leader takes when these circumstances come are what determine the success or failure of the leader. This could be at the board meeting, family meeting among others. Jesus, when the events were no longer comfortable, found Himself wavering, shot back at Himself and the tempter – *"nevertheless not as I will, but as thou (His Father) wilt."* This was where the battle was won and He became a victor. As leaders in whatever capacity, let us learn to catch ourselves when such moments show up so we do not fall off over the cliff.

Friend, Jesus was tempted, He was tested, He came to the head but He stretched himself for more grace to enable Him to fulfill His mission. He refused to throw in the towel but leaned on the everlasting strength of the father. You know what, at that time, the future and destiny of the world, and human race were on a balance, but thank God He did not fail nor disappoint. I plead with every one of us to learn this from Him so as not to disappoint at such times.

Get d' picture!

At the end, He earned Himself a name that is far above all other names both in heaven and earth (Philippians 2:9-11). That is why when you pray in His name things happen; the sick are healed, demons cast out and needs are met. The name gives you access to all things despite your qualifications, so long as you believe. This feat was achieved because He understood what was at stake and the end result. He put in everything and got more than everything in return. When you mention the name of Jesus, demons tremble, things listen and obey.

Contrast Him with King Saul who did not understand the faith God placed on him as the leader of His people, Israel and he disappointed miserably. Most of the assignments God gave him, he did not carry them out to the letter. He picked and chose which to obey. Most people still do this today and rationalize it.

"But Saul and the people spared Agag, and the best of the sheep, and of the oxen, and of the fatlings, and the lambs, and all that was good, and would not utterly destroy them: but everything that was vile and refuse, that they destroyed utterly. Then came the word of the LORD unto Samuel, saying, It repenteth me that I have set up Saul to be king: for he is turned back from following me, and hath not performed my commandments. And it grieved Samuel; and he cried unto the LORD all night." 1 Samuel 15: 9-11 KJV

Most of God's orders were carried out haphazardly as he, his officials and advisers pleased but not according to God's instructions. A lot of people fall culprits here, they would rather disobey God than hurt the feelings of friends, associates and others around them. It has led to God rejecting them without their knowing it. Repent!

Verse 24, "And Saul said unto Samuel, 'I have sinned: for I have transgressed the commandment of the LORD, and thy words: because I feared the people, and obeyed their voice'."

From all the events King Saul surrounded himself with, it was clear he did not understand who he was, who called him and his position as the leader of God's people. He saw himself accountable to the people and not God. A lot of political leaders even some church leaders are in the same shoes as Saul. They are only interested in public opinion and polls, not what God would want them to do to keep the society together under His moral law. Eventually their fate would be like Saul's if they fail to repent. I think Saul's greatest undoing was his inability to be remorseful over his errors, make amends and take corrections.

That ended his rule. And God handed over the baton to a young inexperienced shepherd boy – David, whom He trained and used to deliver His people. From all indication, you will discover that David never disappointed in that duty despite his human failings. God himself even vouched for him.

"And when he had removed him (King Saul), he raised up unto them David to be their king; to whom also he gave their testimony, and said, 'I have found David the son of Jesse, a man after mine own heart, which shall fulfill all my will'." Acts 13:22 KJV

We can learn from this. David learned that act of leadership by being a good follower and obedient servant. If you look at all his accounts, you will discover that in all his steps, God directed him. He

Get d' picture!

went out of his way to ask God where to go, what to do and how to get things done. He received the details and carried them out to the letter. Not that he never failed but he accepted his faults and took responsibility over his actions whenever confronted with them and made amends, which was not the case with his predecessor who would usually rationalize and justify his halfhearted obedience.

When oppositions or obstacles set in

Oppositions and obstacles are sometimes tests. "Does this guy really merit this? Can he handle it? Let's check him out." A lot of times they are temporary setbacks that eventually give way when you persist. When two forces collide, the greater one usually has its way. That is what happens when you are conscious of your personality as you meet with life challenges and oppositions. Refuse to be intimidated, they cannot swallow you.

When you understand who you are, you do not allow temporary setbacks to stop you from reaching your goals. People that persevered relied heavily on the inner strength provided them by the Spirit of God through self-revelation, which He granted them during the trying times. Examples of people that never allowed setbacks to keep them from reaching their goals were Joseph, David, Daniel and others. We know their stories. Those setbacks became platforms for showcasing them to the world.

Joseph, after receiving the revelation of who he was and his purpose, shared the dream with his brothers; they betrayed him. Instead of helping him achieve that purpose, a firestorm of hatred and jealousy were set off that eventually saw his brothers selling him off as a slave. Anyway, we are not looking at what they did to him here but what Joseph did under the unfortunate condition in which he found himself. Perhaps we can learn some things from his actions. He never gave up his dream. Even in the prison he ruled over his mates (Genesis 39:22). The prison experience never made him lose sight of his purpose – leading and solving problems. You will discover that it was through his leadership and problem solving skills that God eventually elevated him from prison to the palace. So friend, do not allow your present condition to make you lose sight of who you are and your purpose. The test is just for a time, eventually you will get through it if you persevere, and also become what you were made to be. The Bible says that the glory that will follow will outweigh any pain or suffering you may have suffered during this process.

Also when David was anointed king over Israel by Prophet Samuel, he was instrumental to killing Goliath of Gath who mocked God and the people of God. His success in that episode saw him became a darling of his people. People began to see him as a treasure to the nation but to Saul, the king, he had become a threat to his throne. As a result, he began to put everything in place to eliminate David.

When this became the case, David ran for his dear life but King Saul pursued after him. Saul was a powerful king, having a great influence in that region at the time. David began to hide from cave to

Get d' picture!

cave, that did not stop the King either; eventually he sought refuge in the enemies' territories (1 Samuel 27:1-4). However, because God was with him, he was preserved. Finally Saul was killed in a battle and the people of Judah took and crowned David king over them, later the entire kingdom followed suit.

A look at the entire episode shows David's wilderness experience as a setback, but that setback could not stop him from being hopeful. Why, you may ask? This was possible because he had gotten the picture of who he was and his purpose in life. The discovery was one; he was also willing to fulfill that purpose. And I want to tell you too, nothing will ever be able to stop you in your life mission and purpose when you discover it and if you stay fast to it. It is only you that can stop you. That could be possible whenever you lose hope and stop pressing forward towards your vision. But God will surely perfect that which concerns you, as long as you are willing to keep going. Always remember that He has promised never to leave nor forsake you (Deuteronomy 31:6). He is always there by your side to see you through every difficulty and bring to reality His promises to you. So, never throw in the towel when you see setbacks or things get tough on the way. Oppositions are indicative of the importance of your pursuits. If your goals are of no value and no threat to the enemy, he will not fight to stop you. So, always stand your ground when they show up, your victory is guaranteed.

From what we read from the above passage, King Saul allowed temporary setback to deny him his destiny. He panicked and pandered to public opinion instead of following the established order and doing what God instructed, when he was faced with a formidable enemy. He did what he was not supposed to do and did not do what he was expected to do; as a result he missed a lifetime opportunity. Remember he told Prophet Samuel on another occasion the people were deserting him and as he saw the enemy approaching, he had no choice but to offer a burnt offering, which as a king, he was not supposed to do.

As for Daniel, he was exceptional in his duties as one of the high ranking officials of King Darius of Persia. As a result, the king wanted to promote and make him the lead officer over other officials. The move did not go down well with other officials and they engineered a plot to stop Daniel. They could not find him lacking in any area as to accuse and blackmail him except that he was a foreigner and serving his God faithfully. As a foreigner, they hated to see him rule over them. They used this dedication to his God to set him up. They plotted and he was thrown into lions' den. Contrary to their anticipation, the lions did not touch nor tear Daniel to pieces, but they were made to have a taste of that plan (Daniel 6). The den experience was a temporary setback but Daniel was not stopped by that, rather he prospered in the land and God was glorified by his faithfulness. This is what God expects from you and me. Stand your ground no matter how hard the situation becomes, even when facing death (Hebrew 12:4). The devil is usually threatened by your successes and achievements - that is why he plots always to subvert them. Never grant him such opportunity nor become an accomplice with him to bring you down.

CHAPTER TWO

How to get understanding

"…; seek and you will find;" Matthew 7:7b

When you are new in a place, business or relationship, you discover that you are not really on top of the game. Sometimes the situation around look overwhelming, especially when vital information is lacking. You grapple with missteps until you are able to figure out things and come to the point that you are in charge, and armed with enough information that helps you handle the situation.

At times like this, some will dare to ask questions, calling people up or agencies and resource groups to find their way around what they want to do. With this route missteps could be minimized.

Also for those not new who are committed to progress, not until one notices that some things are missing or that things are not going normal as expected do they begin to look for the missing items and to finding answers to those things that are not going well. For one to get the needed understanding they have to deliberately engage in seeking knowledge and finding answers towards the things they hope to achieve. It is like a hunter putting on his gear and setting out to hunt for game. It takes careful preparations and selection of the kind of tools you may need in the process. Hunting could be risky. It also involves decisions as to whether or not to engage companions like co-hunters and dogs, the goal – being in the position to catch some prey at the end of the day. That is how to pursue understanding in whatever area of interest; thinking through and making tough decisions to ensure you have all you may need to succeed.

Through learning

The Bible enjoins us to study – 2 Timothy 2:15, search the scriptures – John 5:39. It is the duty of every child of God, especially those that want to get ahead and achieve something meaningful in life, to diligently learn and to find out what the father has laid in stock for them in life through His word. Jesus did that in Luke 4:18-19. When they have been able to discover that, the next step would be to customize their findings to suit them and for their benefits. It is also their duty to discover various steps and principles He has outlined to getting these things done. Take for instance a person who wants to be delivered from lack and poverty. Let us look at what the Bible has to say.

Get d' picture!

"*Those that seeketh, findeth (Matthew 7:8b).*" If the reason you lack or are poor is due to lack of job, onus is on you to go out there and search for jobs. If you have qualifications look for those areas you are qualified to work and apply. If you do not have qualifications, get training that will help you get a job. Learn a vocation, you can be self-employed. God is interested in our working. He promised to bless our work (Psalm 1:3c). These are the things you can discover from the word of God. When you do and apply them in your life, they will help bring change to you. Think about it!

"*In every labor there is profit (Proverbs 14:23).*" This is another step in overcoming lack. When one understands this principle, he will know that folding his arms and looking for handouts does not help him. It does not increase him. It demeans him, especially when the individual is not handicapped. When he puts this to work, eventually he will understand the dignity in labor (Ecclesiastes 9:10) and the blessings that follow.

Some people would rather stay jobless and penniless rather than taking a lower paying job or certain kind of job to meet their needs. To me, that sounds ridiculous. If you can endure the ridicule of not having money to pay your bills and meeting your daily responsibilities, why can you not endure the ridicule of accepting a lower paying (menial) job to get over a hard situation? Which one is better, which is more dignified, having money to meet your needs or being a beggar and not able to meet your obligations? One thing I noticed while in high school doing high jump: you need to back up for a while if you have a big height to scale. Backing up with a purpose does not make you stupid, but it shows your understanding of the sport. The same thing is applicable to life and times (seasons). Same thing when you want to jump up, until you squat down you may never be able to jump high enough. Squatting down to make your leap does not mean you are staying down forever. It only helps you get the needed force and power to jump up to the height you so desire. The same thing happens when life suddenly gets tough, getting a lower paying job to see you through hard time does not mean you accept it and stay there forever. No, it is just to get through the tough time. There will always be that satisfaction when you earn something. At times like this, I have heard testimonies of people like this getting a far better job than the one they lost. When the people that engaged them saw their worth, humility and dedication offered them better positions and salary. Some even go as far as recommending them to friends when they do not have something better to offer them. So every labor has profits hidden in it.

Another principle of unlocking the door of prosperity and success is giving. Check out any addicted giver: they do not lack (Proverbs 11:24-25). Matthew 6:33 says, **"Give, and it shall be given to you good measures pressed down shaken together and running over shall men give to your bossom."** When we learn these principles and do them, our lives will never remain the same but change to the better. So we need to learn all these keys to enable us defeat lack and poverty.

Tithing and more (Malachi 3:10). One cannot overstate the value of tithing and offering. This is one of the places in the scriptures where God specifically asks people to prove Him. People cannot know

Get d' picture!

all these until they settle down to learn and find out these truths and keys to life, which are embedded in the word of God. Applying them to their lives would turn their situations around.

Training

Training requires a trainer; at times you can be your own coach. Here, there is something to be imparted and a goal set to achieving that. Putting into practice whatever you have learned from the Lord will help create a memory and understanding that can never be erased from your mind. When you personally engage in a project or assignment and eventually end it well with results, it kind of drives away every kind of fear or doubt about the possibility of such a thing. Any time you are called up in the future to do the same thing, you do it with more confidence and assurance. I remember when I was learning to drive, I had a lot of anxiety and fear until I first moved the car and drove around the neighborhood with my trainer, even though I had passed the written test. The next day, I drove with much ease. Jesus, after teaching his disciples, set them out two by two to demonstrate and prove what He taught them. Putting the word of God into reality or action and seeing it work for you as the scripture said is what concretizes your understanding and faith in God. Example – giving and receiving, praying for the sick and seeing them healed (Mark 16:16-18) brings the reality of God and His word to you.

Everyone needs this kind of understanding in order to engage properly in his life.

Trial and error

Most inventions we enjoy today came as a result of trial and error. Often when there are no set standards or charted course on a field, scientists and people involved employ trial and error methods to gain some knowledge about the field. This is another way of gaining understanding of things or events around us. Some of us have heard of "drug trials," which manufacturers employ to test the validity of certain manufactured drugs towards a targeted groups or diseases.

I remember also those days when God was teaching me how to recognize and walk with His voice. He would impress something on my spirit or show me some things but instead of doing or carrying out what I was impressed to do, I looked for "matured" believers to ask them what they think. When I heeded their advice against the voice of the Lord, I came back regretting and feeling guilty when their advice failed against God's impression. Eventually I learned to discern, trust and obey that voice. But it was through trials and errors that I learned to do that.

A lot of folks are afraid to fail. As a result they find it hard to try out new things or trying to improve on old stuff. They prefer the status quo to making errors trying something new.

CHAPTER THREE

Where we gain understanding

"The sayings of King Lemuel — an inspired utterance his mother taught him. 'Listen, my son! Listen, son of my womb! Listen, my son, the answer to my prayers! Do not spend your strength on women, your vigor on those who ruin kings. It is not for kings, Lemuel — it is not for kings to drink wine, not for rulers to crave beer, lest they drink and forget what has been decreed, and deprive all the oppressed of their rights. Let beer be for those who are perishing, wine for those who are in anguish! Let them drink and forget their poverty and remember their misery no more. Speak up for those who cannot speak for themselves, for the rights of all who are destitute. Speak up and judge fairly; defend the rights of the poor and needy'." *Proverbs 31: 1-9NIV*

Lemuel was telling of the instructions he received from his mother. As a young believer this passage was very helpful to me. They were the first scriptures God used to teach me about purity and the evil of drunkenness.

From home

Home is the first place the foundation of every child is laid. The success of any child, among other things, depends on the foundation they received from their home; from Mom, Dad and close relatives. In the building and construction world, they believe the foundation of any structure is what determines how strong or solid a structure becomes when finished. That is why they invest heavily in building the foundation. So, folks definitely need to get it right at the home front first in raising their children, if not every other thing becomes patch-up work. The Bible warns against the danger of not getting it right at the onset. *"If the foundation be destroyed, what shall be the hope of the righteous?" (Psalm 11:3 KJV)*

The role of parents is to guide the children in the way they should go so they would succeed, and be able to have a good future. This is done through imbibing the values and culture the family holds dear, to the children. Some of these trainings are verbal, others are not. Some of the values include – hard work, honesty, respect, relationships – those related to you and those not, responsibility and more. Others are the things that are taboo and "no go" areas as far as family is concerned. Where I come from, people are usually mindful of the family name. When I was young, when you visited a relation or even in school because we lived in a close-knit community where everyone knew each other, as a kid if you misbehaved or showed laziness or disrespect, you would be called out on it and your family would be told. The same thing happened when you were a good kid. I remember several occasions, running into someone and being asked, "Are you the son of so and so?" When I answered yes, they usually said, "You look like your mom and smile like her," then they would tell me how they knew my mom and her virtues. These are the things family helps us receive free of charge.

These are the things that fashion our lives as we begin to engage the world outside our homes. The Bible attests to this. ***"Train a child in the way he should go, when he grows up would not depart from it" (Proverbs 22:6).*** How we relate to our surroundings is in part due to the training we received from our various homes; the same thing happens when there are issues in our lives. The way we saw our parents handle issues that came their way would most likely be the way we are going to tackle and address such matters if they show up again in our lives. Look at the story of Abraham and Isaac, at difficult times in their lives they set out to go to Egypt and other things they did when that time showed up (Genesis 26:2).

It is at the family level that children begin to understand how things work in life. There is a popular saying where I come from, **"When the mother goat is chewing the cord, the offspring would be watching."** Children are copycats and tend to copy every action of the parents. When we were kids we usually played "House." Once our parents left the house, our friends would come over. We took every role from father to mother and all that. In that mock home, you acted out the role that was assigned to you or whichever you could do very well. If mom nagged, you mimicked that, if dad was a bully, you did the same. It used to be a lot of fun. It was only when they caught us unexpectedly that they found us in the act. Most times you saw them laughing. Kids are very intelligent. I remember a story told about a young boy whose father was a pastor. He usually saw his father ministering to people, especially the sick, when they came to see him. One day, while the father was away, his mother became sick and lay in bed. The young boy looked and did not find his father, but he saw the coat where Dad usually hung his ministry suits. The boy, being small, arranged some chairs and climbed up and took his father's coat and put it on. He went to his sick mother's bed and began to pray for her as the father would. The story went that the mother recovered. But the lesson is that he did what he saw his father do when such situations arose. This is the same thing that happens in dysfunctional families, too. The children will surely act out what they observe from dad and mom. There is another saying, *"An apple does not fall far from the tree."*

Parents should do everything within their power to give their children a solid foundation that will stand the test of time and in the long run, bring glory not only to the child but also to them as parents.

It is in the family that children learn honesty, to love and sacrifice. It is there they learn to lead, work hard, protect, take responsibilities, learn accountability and patriotism. Whatever is not learned at home is usually hard to learn in the outside world. We have a saying in Igbo culture that you can safely direct the yam tendril only

Get d' picture!

when it is still tender, if you try to direct or redirect it when it is no longer tender the tendril will break. This same thing applies to raising children the way we would want them to grow. Once children start to develop their will and form their own opinion, it becomes hard to direct and redirect them. Most of the delinquent children, even adults we have today roaming in our society are in part due to parental failures in training their wards. Our society today is the reflection of our homes – violence and hypocrisy.

Parents know their children better than anyone else, including the children themselves. They know their abilities and strengths. That is why they are in the very best position to train and direct the children to navigate life and succeed in it. During the developmental stages of these children, the onus is on the parents to direct in decision making, as these children cannot make some trusted and informed choices about their lives. This helps to prevent "had I known" situations from arising in the future.

I know a guy whose father wanted him to study Electrical and Electronics Engineering at the University but he blew it. He recommended that field to him because he took time to understudy the young man and discovered where he would do very well in life and where he was a natural fit. But the guy thought otherwise and has regretted it since.

Many young people fail in life because their parents do not see them as a priority. Children are no longer as important as career or personal ambitions. Some even play some family politics with their children and so do little to channel them in the right part of life to follow. The majority of those that eventually succeed, do so through trial and error and those that played catch-up along the way.

As a child, my mother would pack my school bag with everything I would need for the day before I went to school. Also, she would open my bag when I returned from school and I had to account for all the pencils, sharpeners, erasers and other things found in my bag that she did not put there nor buy for me. I had to explain when I became a custodian of other people's stuff found in my bag. Those interrogations and the experiences were never funny. Some of you whose mothers were old school will understand what I am saying. It made me sit up; always crosscheck myself and return whatever I borrowed that was not mine before heading home from school. She would also check my classwork to see if I was up-to-date and also ensure I did my assignments promptly. She checked to prevent me from any form of truancy in my school and class activities. She yearned for an honest and hardworking child. When I grew up, she was proud of me. I want to tell you that I have missed her since she passed on to be with the Lord.

Community and Environment

Our community and environment also play a great role in determining what we become in life. That is what some call culture. There are some generally acceptable and unacceptable norms. This determines how we see and perceive things, people and react when certain things happen whether they are far or near. Some of the things that compose our community and environment that I want to look at are schools, media and the church. Apart from our home or immediate family, these are other groups that have tremendous influence over our understanding of life and who we are. They help shape the way we think and behave. If you are from an egalitarian society, it is very likely that you will exhibit that character in your dealings in life. The same thing will happen when the individual comes from ultra conservative culture. It is also likely that you see things from any of these perspectives if you happen to come from any of them.

1. From school

This is the place that helps develop our intellects, educate us about ourselves and also the way we see things that surround us. The teachers here use their acquired knowledge and skills including life experiences to guide the student into the intricate issues of life, career and future. The teacher employs subjects with curriculum to unveil more complex things about life to the individual (student). Eventually, the knowledge and understanding the individual is able to garner here go a long way to equip him and help make him whatever he chooses to become in life.

2. Media

Every day the media keeps bombarding the public with loads of information. There are those that are relevant and helpful to the needs of the people while others are not. Most of the things we hear and see day in and day out from the media outlets have some direct influence over what our lives become. That is why it is important to be mindful of what you and your children consume while watching the television or movies. The Bible warns that we guard our hearts with all diligence because that is where the springs of life come from (Proverbs 4:23). Whatever goes through our eyes and ears ends up in our hearts. From the heart, those things begin to exert control over us after we must have processed them.

There is also the social media – Facebook, YouTube, Twitter, among others. Some parents have of late discovered that their children become brainwashed or deceived over some important issues of their lives as a result of what they see and consume daily from these media platforms. Some of the crimes and violence, even perversions rampant today in the society came as a result of what people filled their minds with while watching movies and these other media outlets.

3. The Church

The church should keep up with providing the needed moral compass for the society as it has done since ages. But if you look closely at the moment, you will not be in doubt that it is failing in this responsibility, and not fulfilling this duty. As a result, there is no longer a moral yardstick to look up to as a people; the entire moral horizon now looks at best hazy. A situation where church leaders are even confused about some social issues that the Bible clearly stated is really disturbing. As this is the case, the church has really not provided that needed leadership. Jesus, when He was addressing his followers during the "Sermon on the Mount", warned the church against losing her role in the society. According to Him, ***"You are the salts of the earth, and when the salt loses its taste, of what use would it be? It would be thrown out and trampled underfoot." (Matthew 5:13)***. I think that is where the church is headed today, unless something drastic happens to awaken her from the deep slumber she found herself in. You may have been hearing the clamor for the church to start paying taxes and be held accountable for certain things. What does this tell you? The church is losing its taste and clout, also becoming irrelevant to a vast number of people.

When the church does its duty, the society exhibits high morals and love; there is also trust and protection. You also see these rubbing off on the kids who through the things they learned build a healthy society in the future. The church needs to step up its activities, especially towards the younger generations because the teachings and things they learn will also help determine their sense of value and direction. Let us take the following counsel serious if the church really wants to make a comeback.

"You are the light of the world. A town built on a hill cannot be hidden. Neither do people light a lamp and put it under a bowl. Instead they put it on its stand, and it gives light to everyone in the house. In the same way, let your light shine before others, that they may see your good deeds and glorify your Father in heaven." Matthew 5:14-16 NIV

Our places of work

Another place individuals gain understanding is in their place of work. The regular training (both job related and social skills) and work activities are great avenues of empowering people with needed information and experience that will be helpful for them to succeed in life.

The driving and safety training I received when I got a job with Chevron was very helpful. The benefits are invaluable. I am able to drive safely on the highway; reduce the risks of accidents, reduce my

Get d' picture!

insurance premium, reduce the wear and tear on my vehicle and more. It has been a win-win situation.

There are many other things people learn from their workplaces. Some people that transition to own their businesses later in life sometimes learned those skills from their original workplace (the company they worked for). I know a lot of people who did that. The list is endless. All you need to do is to open your eyes and see opportunities that abound in your workplace and learn something that will be of great benefit to you, and perhaps your community.

CHAPTER FOUR

Benefits of having good understanding

Self confidence

When you know who you are, you will know how to behave and how to carry yourself as you walk or speak. When you look at our soldiers, you will find out that they do not behave like ordinary citizens. They are disciplined and mature despite their age. They are usually courteous and respectful, even in the community. They are also protective, perhaps due to their training. That is what understanding of who you are brings into your life. Like one of the Boy Scout rules, they are always prepared, to defend the land and its people. They sense danger and prevent it. Three American officers displayed their bravery when they foiled a terror

Get d' picture!

attack on a Paris bound train in France mid-August, 2015 while on their vacation. They could do that because they were trained and also understood their purpose. Hundreds of other people were there but could not detect nor avert the danger.

Excellence

With good understanding of yourself, you are in position to quickly know what you have enormous grace and strength to accomplish with ease and excellence. With that also you give it all you got. You do not allow yourself to be bogged down by things that are not relevant to your purpose, especially those beyond your capacity. Neither should you be engaging in things below your capacity if your hallmark is excellence. You should do things that are commensurate to your strength to show the stuff you are made of. When Apostle Paul discovered his purpose, he laid aside those things that were no longer relevant to that mission.

"Yea doubtless, and I count all things but loss for the excellency of the knowledge of Christ Jesus my Lord: for whom I have suffered the loss of all things, and do count them but dung, that I may win Christ." Philippians 3:8 KJV

With that done, he focused his attention on fulfilling that single purpose. That was why he had a terrific result in his ministry. You can too, when you discipline yourself to focus on what matters. All you need to do when you find out your purpose is to clear the clutter on your to do list and launch your entire energy on that one important thing. I remember reading an article about Tiger Woods one time; he reportedly said he does not know how to do any other thing but golf. His success in the sport was that he gave all his life to it. He succeeded. Look at Serena Williams, J.J. Watts and others doing that one thing they are good at.

A lot of people are not achieving commensurate results to their abilities in their areas of calling because they are not willing to let go of things that are not related or relevant to fulfilling their purpose. They still want to play around with those habits, those friends, vocations that they do not need. They want to juggle them all along. As a result, those things become distractions or unnecessary loads that eventually if care is not taken kill the mission.

A lady reportedly testified how her life was turned around once she decided to give heed to her inner voice and passion. As a trained lawyer representing clients in various court cases and succeeding in life and career, she keeps feeling a void inside and no satisfaction with her job. But she discovered that she fantasizes about interior decorations a lot, especially when with clients. At times, before leaving an office after meeting with clients in their office, she would sketch a fitting furniture set that would match the office or the place she visited. She would also figure out the type of curtain and painting that would match the place. This led her to discuss the issue with her pastor as it became a concern to her. According to her, the pastor told her, "If that's the way you feel about it, go for it. That may be where your destiny lies." I think before then, she already had met with a carpenter, whom she

Get d' picture!

showed those designs, who was skilled and willing to build them according her specifications. Then she launched, formed a business and resigned from her law practice. According to her story, in less than one year she had made what she would not have made in all her entire career as a lawyer.

Friend, you cannot continue to "manage" life. It is time to live your life to the fullest; enough of just getting by. Find out who you are, find out your talents; discover the problems you were created to solve. You are not just occupying space, you were made for something. That assignment is waiting for you; it is what will distinguish you in this life. That service is what will announce and bring you prosperity in life. It is an honor and blessing to serve and solve problems.

Favor and progress

One thing I discovered in life is that help usually comes one's way when he or she begins to engage in those things they are good at and that are beneficial to the community. There they see a lot of volunteers and various support coming their way.

Knowing when and where to stop

A lot of people do not know when they have reached their limit, when and where to stop an ongoing action or process to avoid unpleasant circumstances. Some keep going and at the end of the day, they regret it. Take, for instance, in a home where there is a sharp disagreement between spouses, the wife snapped and began to verbally attack her husband. A man of understanding would know when to step out of the place or house to douse the tension. It does not matter if you are right. Wisdom is what prevails at this time, not right. It could be the other way around and the wife leaves. It is when the atmosphere has been restored to normalcy that you can make that point. You should know when you are approaching your endurance limit, give peace a chance and avoid any foolish actions. Some may take it as weakness but it is not, rather it shows strength. The Bible talks about self-control – a fruit of the Spirit: one being able to have rule over his emotions. It is the higher that looks out for the lower in grace. But the man that lacks understanding will do the reverse and end up paying the penalties, which may be very costly.

Some people want to buy a house, some want to establish their own businesses or make other financial investments but they find it hard to control their appetites to enable them have some savings for down payments or outright payments.

"He that loveth pleasure shall be a poor man: he that loveth wine and oil shall not be rich." Proverbs 21:17 KJV

If having a good future is your dream, you have to learn how to say no to unnecessary spending and your appetite. You have to learn financial discipline and focus on your goals. Some people are earning the same thing you are earning but are able to squeeze things out and

Get d' picture!

save for a rainy day. Why would you remain on deficit every month cycle? Put on your thinking cap, you can do better than that.

Also, how can you have a beautiful home when you are not devoted to making it that way? You only reap whatever you sow in life. It is time to stop troubling your home, learn to face your demons. It is time to start investing your love, emotion, strength and time to make your home what you want to see it become. How many times do you stay back to support your spouse and kids at their difficult times or is it just about you? How many times do you go out of your way to create something memorable in their lives? Is it only when they make mistakes that you pounce on them? What about family time, have you ever had time to play with the kids, go to games or picnics with them? How about story time? How do you treat your spouse; respectfully or as an inconvenience? Or is it all about your job and business? Say no to every form of distractions and deceptions. The problem is not your spouse or the children, it is you. Once you change your attitude and perceptions, the change you anticipated will follow.

Some people wonder why they do not command the power of God despite all the church rituals like fasting and prayers they faithfully engage themselves in. They forget that lack of passion for the things of God and those hidden sins they condone and commit are the accursed things in their lives. Some of them engage in pornography and all manner of immoral acts and behaviors. Some intentionally cheat to get ahead. How do you expect God to show up in a defiled temple? You need to first purge yourself of every form of defilement for Him to show up, He is a holy God. The Bible says if any man purges himself of all these (sins), he becomes a vessel unto honor, prepared for the master's (God's) use.

"Nevertheless the foundation of God standeth sure, having this seal, The Lord knoweth them that are his. And, let everyone that nameth the name of Christ depart from iniquity. But in a great house there are not only vessels of gold and of silver, but also of wood and of earth; and some to honour, and some to dishonour. If a man therefore purge himself from these, he shall be a vessel unto honour, sanctified, and meet for the master's use, and prepared unto every good work." 2 Timothy 2:19-21 KJV

Also, not knowing who they are and their limits are reasons people abuse substances. Drunks, addicts, perverts and others do not know who they are and when they have crossed the line. Some do not even know how to say no to their appetite. However, good understanding helps you know when you have reached your limit and when to say "no" to further pressure. One thing I have found is that many people, including believers, at times find it hard to say no even when they know they have reached that point. They keep on taking up things. They want to please people. They do not consider being faithful to any commitment they may enter an issue anymore. This could be found in work places, especially where people do eye service. Because these sets are before their boss or supervisor they want to please, they put more work on their plates even when it is clear to them they would not be able to deliver. At the end, they complain and murmur when things do not go well, which the Bible warns us against. Common

Get d' picture!

sense, they say, is not all that common. If they also mess things up, they are held accountable. The Bible warns us against overestimating ourselves.

"For I say, through the grace given unto me, to every man that is among you, not to think of himself more highly than he ought to think; but to think soberly, according as God hath dealt to every man the measure of faith." Romans 12:3 KJV

Beloved, discover your limits and know when and where to stop and say "NO" to issues, to help you enjoy the peace of God as you navigate this life. It is well with you.

CHAPTER FIVE

Discovering you

The word of God, the Bible is the mirror of life and resource field where an individual can discover who he is. It has all the information one may ever need about themselves and anything they may think of. Once the individual consults with it daily, like a woman would at a mirror every morning and every time she wants to reassure herself about her looks, they will continue to discover and see themselves in clearer terms. Eventually, they never remain the same and no longer walk in the dark of ignorance anymore. It is like a resource field where a careful and diligent explorer harvests troves of treasure that would change his entire life forever. The Bible is a life manual every living being needs in order to succeed. It empowers the person about them, and God's purpose about them. Someone certainly

Get d' picture!

needs to know who they really are to enable them actually and fully operate on the level they are made to be in life.

I remember one story in my community about a hunter who went hunting and found an eagle's egg. When he got home, he put the egg with one of his hens that was sitting on (incubating) its eggs to hatch. After sitting on the eggs for a time the eggs hatched; the chickens and the eagle emerged and began to move about together scratching the ground to feed on earthworms and dirt. This continued that way over time until one day as the eagle, now a bit grown, saw a bird like it flying over the sky. It was attracted to that sight and envied the bird, but felt it could do the same. It tried and found it could fly too. It was very hilarious. It tried again and again and found it does not belong to the ground and should not be feeding on dirt and earthworms. The eagle flew away to begin a new life when it discovered who it was. It broke off from what it was used to and away from every hindrance into what it was foreordained to be – could no longer be limited.

This is like many people I meet day-by-day. Their problem is that they have refused to look up like the eagle to see who they really are and where they can be, so they keep feeding on the crumbs – the dirt of life, they keep operating below their potential and are not able to fulfill their purpose and destiny. Some of you that are reading this book, this may be your story, but you need to get up and take some action. Look up! Perhaps your background is being a drag on you, the family you came from or your environment? You can beat these things once you understand who you are. That is the essence of the word of God and this book, to help you see you and also to be who you are supposed to be. Once you get this picture you are unstoppable.

a. Who am I?

It is good for believers to start seeing themselves the way God sees them. I remember from the account of the Bible, when the Midianites oppressed the people of Israel; the people started hiding to avoid being spotted by the enemy. If they wanted to harvest and process their crops, they did under the cover of the night to avoid any form of attention. This tells you the type of humiliation and oppression the people of God were subjected to by their oppressors. It could also be likened to today for so many believers in many different countries where identifying as a Christian makes you a target of crime, persecution and killing (beheading). That was the time an angel of the Lord appeared to Gideon and said, "O mighty man of valor! (Judges 6:12-16)" Gideon would have said, "Oh, Man – why set me up like this. Are you a new dude in town? (In my place they will say JJC – Jonny just come.) It's like you don't know who now owns the jungle?" and many more.

But from the angel's proclamation, you will understand that God does not see you how you see yourself and the circumstances surrounding you, nor the way others see you. He sees you as a finished product. A baby boy on his mother's lap is potentially a man, even though he is still in the process. When Rebekah was pregnant with Esau and Jacob, God told her two nations were in her womb (Genesis 25:23). You are a work in progress in His hand, which He is perfecting to show the world, so do not sabotage it. You may be weak today but God is saying you are a mighty man of valor. You may be sick but God is seeing a valiant warrior, a terror to the kingdom of darkness. You may look poor but God is seeing that wealthy person He will use to feed the poor and carry the good news of the gospel to the ends of the world. God does not see things as humans do (Isaiah 55:8-9). Believers need to start getting their minds renewed and restructured again by reading and studying the word of God.

What do you do when your PC is corrupted and the hard drive running below par? Experts advise that you either buy a new one or reformat the one you have. Since you cannot buy a new mind, you can reformat it by the word of God. This is what the mind needs at intervals to enable it to maintain its edge to function effectively.

Believers also need to cap it up with prayer and needed actions. They should stop feeding themselves with junks from the televisions and movies, and other unnecessary gossip outlets and friends. By constantly looking into this perfect law of liberty, (The word of God) they will begin to think as God would, and also appreciate and reflect what He wants to achieve in their lives. As we do this, let us start seeing us the way God sees us.

1. Once an individual gives his or her life to Christ, they become the children of God. In John 1:12 the Bible says, ***"But as many as received him, to them gave he power to become the sons of God, even to them that believe on his name." KJV.*** Every child born to a human being becomes a human being. Offspring of animals are animals; if a goat gives birth to an offspring it is called a goat. I do not know why it is hard for the children of God to be called gods. Even Jesus said ye are gods. ***(Jesus answered them, 'Is it not written in your law, I said, Ye are gods?' John 10:34)***. Also in Psalm 82:6 the Bible says this, ***"I have said, 'Ye are gods; and all of you are children of the most High'."*** Children born to princes are by default princes. Take for instance Prince Charles of the UK, who had two sons – William and Harry. Both these guys are princes. Even Prince William's young son, George is being addressed as a prince. So if one is born unto God, he automatically becomes a god. Just like these princes were taught how to grow and be a prince, every child of God needs to be taught how to grow and become gods wherever they found themselves.

In 2 Corinthians 5:17 Apostle Paul said, ***"If any man be in Christ he is a new creation, old things have passed away. Behold all things have become new."***

New creation here means that the nature of God has been infused in him, that nature (seed of life) that supersedes the power of his human flesh. This is why when a person gets born again he begins to have dominion over his flesh. There you see drunkards, sex perverts and killers becoming sober and genuine lovers. What every believer needs to do is to start reflecting the God nature in them so as to impact others around them. This will help usher in the needed change in our communities and society. Jesus said that that which is born of the flesh is flesh, but that which is born of the Spirit is spirit (John 3:6). Also remember that Apostle Paul in Romans 8:14-17 said,

"For as many as are led by the Spirit of God, they are the sons of God. For ye have not received the spirit of bondage again to fear; but ye have received the Spirit of adoption, whereby we cry, Abba, Father. The Spirit itself beareth witness with our spirit, that we are the children of God: And if children, then heirs; heirs of God, and joint-heirs with Christ; if so be that we suffer with him, that we may be also glorified together." KJV

Paul also said in Hebrew 2:11 that Jesus called believers his brethren ***(For both he that sanctifieth and they who are*** *sanctified are all of one: for which cause he is not ashamed to call them brethren.)*

The essence of these explanations is to help you understand your position or who you are once you become a child of God or born again into God's family, and not be kicked around by the devil and his agents due to ignorance. You are expected to live out this truth for the world to see. The Bible says my people are destroyed for lack of knowledge (Hosea 4:6).

We need to start seeing ourselves the way God sees us. This is to enable us become who He has made us to be. We cannot afford to continue to see ourselves differently. If we are the children of God as the scriptures say, then we are gods (Psalm 82:6). We need to begin to understand it; perceive ourselves that way and also start acting that way to help us become exactly that. Those days my mother would usually give me this quote, "**The secret of playing a part was to think yourself into it. You could never keep it up unless you could convince yourself you were it.**" I later discovered that this was from Nicholas Rankin's book on how the British won the two world wars. Applying it to ourselves, we need to start thinking and convince ourselves that we are what the Bible or the word of God says we are if we want to be victorious in life. Find out the attributes of

God, start imbibing and imitating those (Ephesians 5:1). Jesus said He did not do anything of His own, but whatever He saw the father do (John 5:19). If God says I am His son, I should start saying that too and also seeing myself in that light, if He says I am a new creation, I have to convince myself that that is what I am. Also, I should start seeing myself that way and also living that way, I do not need to allow my former errors; weaknesses or ignorance and what people say determine who I am to God. That my son misbehaved or disappointed me does not invalidate his humanity nor make him not to be my child anymore. There may be a break in fellowship but he is still my child. All he needs to do is repent, confess and repair the fellowship. This same thing applies to our relationship with God. As we discipline our children when they fall short so does God to us when we err to enable us get back on track.

It was because my mother told me that I am the son of my father that I believed. As a result, I not only bear his name I also assert ownership over all he owned and left behind. I do not beg for them, rather I take and exercise authority over them. I also give them to whoever I want. As occasions demand I equally declare it that I am his son. When my father was there, also I created a relationship with him that endeared us to each other. That is how it should be between us and God. We need to understand Him and enjoy the benefits of that relationship. Like my mother, the Bible is telling us the same thing – we are children of God.

Then, if actually I am God's child I should start living that out and make it a reality. The Bible says that the entire world is waiting for your manifestation.

"For the creation waits in eager expectation for the children of God to be revealed." Romans 8:19 NIV

They are tired of all words without action, clouds without rain and all noise without substance. They want to see the sons of God in action, bringing the glory and authority of God to bear in their neighborhoods as Jesus did hundreds of years ago. It is not about being arrogant as some may be thinking. No! Jesus was never arrogant despite knowing who He was. However, He used that knowledge with compassion to bring salvation and deliverance to His people and the needy. That is what the entire creation desperately yearns for now.
When you go to several churches today, despite various activities, after church service the people will go back home and still remain the same. Would that be the case if Jesus were here? I think this should be the question. Is there a missing link between what Jesus did then and what we do now? You discover that despite all the choreographies,

acrobatics and semantics that filled the service, the people remain untouched by God and go back home the same way they came. It is like going to a restaurant and at the end going home hungry with an empty stomach for not finding food to eat. Under this scenario what do you expect from the people? Dearth and ignorance of spiritual matters and lack of power of God is what follows.

Sometimes I ask myself, is it that the word of God has expired, as most things in the world markets today have expiration dates, or that the practitioners are not getting it right? I think the latter is the case because I still see God answer my prayers. Remember Jesus said, **"Greater works shall ye do than these (things He did) because I go to the father" (John 14:12).** Why are we not seeing these in our time? Heaven expects us to do much more than Jesus did before returning there. The Bible says that forever the word of God is settled in heaven (Psalm 119:89), so it cannot have expired. Perhaps there may have been some elements of adulteration because what is coming out of some pulpits today is mindboggling. There have been efforts by so many false prophets (agents of Satan) parading themselves now as men of God, who have infiltrated the church today, to hoodwink the gullible. In Matthew 24:4b Jesus, while answering the disciples about the signs of the end and of His return, warned them strongly against deception, **"Take heed (be careful, be observant) that no man deceive you."** I enjoin every serious believer to seek the truth, study the scriptures and do not joke about them. Your soul is at stake. The devil is seriously bargaining for your soul. The Berea church were not deceived by the eloquence of their preachers (Acts 17:11). Whatever they heard they went and did some "fact checks" to ensure it was in line with the scriptures before believing, but today the reverse is the case. Many children of God no longer read the scriptures for themselves. If you ask them they complain about time, stress, work and family. Hope God's blessings are not becoming a curse or stumbling to you. They only depend on what the pastors say. Most now would tell you, "Pastor said this, Pastor said that," but not "The Bible says." No wonder they do not know when the man of God has lost steam and started to derail, they fall headlong with him. They are not even informed enough to help the pastor to get back on track. We need to get back the passion and be what God wants us to be here and also carry out our individual and collective assignments. We can do it. It only takes willingness and action on our side and God would do the rest.

When He told the people of Israel He had given them the land of Canaan, all they needed to do was to see themselves in the land or take over the land. With that mental picture created, then plot a strategy to conquer and take over the land. The naked truth was that He was there with them to see they succeeded in doing just that. But they were blinded to that truth. The same thing is applicable to us today. Any promises God made you are yours to take, but you need to start seeing yourself take hold of them as God says, start acting them out as He would. If you go with that mindset and disposition, you see yourself manifesting His nature. How can one do that? You can definitely do that by renewing your mind.

Renew your mind

To effectively grasp what God has made you to be, you need to totally clear or renew your mind of clutter of things from the depraved world. Human minds are powerful but have been influenced by limitations and distortions emanating from their surroundings. There is junk that has accessed and continues to access human minds. Unless these things are detoxed and access stopped, we may not be able to clearly think and see as God sees, and as long as that is the case there will continue to be limitations that hinder our advancements and progress in life. The Bible says we are what we think.

"For as he thinketh in his heart, so is he:" Proverbs 23:7 KJV

The "I can'ts, it's impossibles, and I'm afraids, my pains, my sicknesses, my anger or my hot temper" lexes are things we learned from our environments that limit us. It is not just that we learned them but we have customized them; we own and declare them time and time again every day, sometimes consciously and unconsciously. They are the things that undermine the divinity in you but we can reverse them. The Bible warns against conforming to them.

"And be not conformed to this world: but be ye transformed by the renewing of your mind, that ye may prove what is that good, and acceptable, and perfect, will of God." Romans 12:2

The word of God is the detoxing element and a shield (Ephesians 6:16). It cleanses from accumulated junk and protects you from further assaults.

"Sanctify them through thy truth: thy word is truth." John 17:17

When your mind is renewed it becomes easy to see clearly and understand. When that happens the mental picture of what you see becomes easy to pursue. When an architect conceives a mental picture of what he wants to see, he draws that on a paper, the same thing with a civil engineer who wants to construct a bridge, an entrepreneur that wants to build an enterprise or a missionary who wants to save a people from eternal damnation. With time and resources they bring those things into existence. Most magnificent structures you see scattered over the entire scape of the Earth, businesses, medical discoveries and others are results of mental pictures developed by founders of such endeavors. As an architect conceives and draws some of these great edifices we see littered everywhere that is how God expects us to see who we are in Him and start manifesting ourselves to this world we find ourselves, so they can see.

What I discovered is that folks dwell so much on their weaknesses, things that do not work and other negative stuffs around them instead of things that work, their strength and the things they want to see happen in their lives. They beat themselves up, not just beating up but beating themselves into pulp over an issue that has not worked or turned out as they wanted; things like getting out of shape, rejected in a relationship, lost a job or got disappointed. Before you know it, worry sets in and the whole thing begins to spiral out of control. But these things are not the things that define you. You should be smarter than that. Get this picture; you are a child of God!

Others make the same error. It is good to be remorseful and genuinely repent whenever one fails, but joining the devil to torment yourself is what I do not agree with. Even when God has forgotten you made an error, some keep recounting it and keep running round in a circle rather than moving forward. Some people are even so hard on themselves that they can kill or commit suicide. When you fall, get up, clean yourself up and move forward. Jesus told the adulterous woman, **"Go and sin no more."** He never asked her to go and keep worrying about her sin. So friend, keep moving forward; do not stay where you fell. Falling is evidence of one coming short of his original state. Error is also proof of one departing from his perfect position. All these show a departure from God's nature residing in you. But you need to get up from there and move forward to where you should be.

Most of the business empires you see today scattered everywhere and raking in billions of dollars in interests are being sustained by the effects of wrong thinking and perception of people. Mental homes and psychiatric hospitals are filled up today due to that. Also pharmaceutical companies are expanding.
Depression, low self-esteem and feeling of rejection, even suicide are all products of wrong thinking – people not knowing who they are, thinking all manner of thoughts, and

it is taking a great toll. When you understand who you are and start thinking that way, you will begin to subdue your circumstances. Like Moses, you will become a god to those situations.

2. You are a king.

"And hath made us kings and priests unto God and his Father; to him be glory and dominion for ever and ever. Amen." Rev. 1:6 KJV

Once you become a Born Again Believer, heaven begins to recon you as a king. As a result, you start to exert dominion over things around you. When you speak, power is released, because the Bible says that where the word of the king is there is power (Ecclesiastes 8:4). Remember also what Jesus said in Matthew 18:18, *"Verily I say unto you, whatsoever ye shall bind on earth shall be bound in heaven: and whatsoever ye shall loose on earth shall be loosed in heaven."* That is why when you speak and make pronouncements you see it come to be. When you pray for people you see healings, miracles and demons cast out.

Every king has a kingdom or domain. As a believer your domain is the earth here.

"And hast made us unto our God kings and priests: and we shall reign on the earth." Rev. 5:10 KJV

As a believer your sphere of influence is anywhere on this earth. Do not allow the enemy to cower you that you cannot do a thing over issues that are important to you. The Bible says, **"And you shall decree a thing and it shall be established unto you." (Job 22:28).** You may be in need of a job, good health, good home or success in life. It may be good marriage, career, good retirement benefits or name it, the scripture says, "and you shall decree a thing and it shall be established unto you." Therefore open your mouth and start unleashing your power and authority as a king over your circumstances. I have never seen a king beg, not even in the poorest of nations. They have set privileges no matter the condition of things around. That is what you are. Start exploiting that advantage and see your life turn around to good. God is waiting and the angels are ready. Do not bungle this opportunity, you have it on a platter, utilize it and see yourself be where you are made and designed to be.

3. You are a priest

In addition to being a king, you are also a priest. Priests offer sacrifices to God. It is not just that you are a priest; you became a royal priest when you become a believer in

Christ (1 Peter 2:9-10). Priests have access to God. As a priest you should know the type of sacrifices God accepts, when and how to perform them. You also should know how to select the kind of sacrifice He likes. The essence of the sacrifices is to praise and worship the Lord; being able to appreciate Him for who He is and all He keeps doing.

As a priest your duty also is to present the people in your domain and their needs to God. Some may be having difficulties and need divine help, as a priest you are obligated to seek help for them from God and to see that they received the needed helps. Priests serve as intermediaries between God and man.
Priests should also intercede and pray for the success and peace of the nations and places in which they find themselves, especially during difficult times. They should also pray for the leadership of those places for wisdom, humility and fear of God as they make policies and take decisions that affect the people.

"I have set watchmen upon thy walls, O Jerusalem, which shall never hold their peace day nor night: ye that make mention of the LORD, keep not silence, And give him no rest, till he establish, and till he make Jerusalem a praise in the Earth." Isaiah 62:6-7 KJV

As a believer you are a watchman having oversight over the things that happen in your domain. You make and enforce change by reporting back to heaven through intercessions and prayers. Knowing you have all these influences at your disposal, you do not need to be prodded up and down to explore them to your advantage and also change your world. Learn to motivate yourself or self-motivate and pray. With your various prayers, you move the hand of God to doing exceptional things.

Praying is like a construction worker standing out there using a remote in his hand manipulating the crane to lift an incredible construction load off the ground to a 50-story high building or a dockworker lifting massive containers off the ship with the help of a crane being operated by a joystick. Ordinarily you know he could not do that with his physical force or energy. That is the way prayer works. The cranes are like the hand of God while the remote and joystick our prayers.

When you understand the power of prayer, as a believer you will start engaging it daily in every aspect of your life. With that you cannot be limited.

4. You are a soldier

Every soldier's duty is to protect the territorial integrity of his nation and save his own people from external aggression and extinction. In the United States for example, a soldier in the U.S. Army is tasked with upholding the Constitution and protecting the country's freedom. This same thing is applicable to every believer; your duty is to fight to keep the faith alive, also to propagate and protect the ideals of the kingdom. The Bible enjoins us to fight the good fight of faith (1 Timothy 6:12). It is a fight even though the weapons of our warfare are not carnal (2 Corinthians 10:4). Also in the book of Jude verse 3, the Bible enjoins us to contend earnestly (sincerely, intensely, seriously) for the faith given to us. This is not a child's play. There is ongoing war between the kingdom of light and the kingdom of darkness. And as a soldier of light, your duty is to defend the faith and ensure that the faith is not muscled or stamped out of human space. Preach the gospel, live the gospel, do not allow anyone to cower you into backing down from propagating this good news. You are obligated to be on the vanguard of projecting it and never backing down to the antics of the enemy.

As this war rages on, Apostle Paul enjoined every believer to be strong, not on the account of their own flesh but on the might that comes from the Almighty. He further advised on what it takes to be this great soldier and be successful.

"Put on the whole armour of God, that ye may be able to stand against the wiles of the devil. For we wrestle not against flesh and blood, but against principalities, against powers, against the rulers of the darkness of this world, against spiritual wickedness in high places. Wherefore take unto you the whole armour of God that ye may be able to withstand in the evil day, and having done all, to stand. Stand therefore, having your loins girt about with truth, and having on the breastplate of righteousness. And your feet shod with the preparation of the gospel of peace. Above all, taking the shield of faith, wherewith ye shall be able to quench all the fiery darts of the wicked. And take the helmet of salvation, and the sword of the Spirit, which is the word of God: Praying always with all prayer and supplication in the Spirit, and watching thereunto with all perseverance and supplication for all saints." Ephesians 6:11-18 KJV

Arming yourself with this truth and daily applying them in all you do positions you as a person for victory in this life's affairs (battle). So the time you are in is not the time to relax but a time for more diligence. There is a reward, it is eternal and of great value. If the people of this world could risk their lives for that which has no eternal value, I think we much more need diligence. God bless!

As believers there are lots of things the Bible reveals concerning us. The scripture says we are the begotten of God (Psalm 2:7-9), new creation (2 Corinthians 5:17), kingdom priests (1 Peter 2:9), light of the world, Christ Ambassadors (2 Corinthians 5:20), co-Heirs with Christ, redeemed, translated (Colossians 1:13), blessed, not cursed.

Friend, this truth is not revealed to make you cocky or arrogant but to help you become bold to keep and maintain the estate entrusted into your hands by the Almighty. Many are being destroyed because they do not know this. You should not be in that statistic.

CHAPTER SIX

Discovering your purpose

Purpose is the reason for which something is done or created, or for which something or someone exists. It could be expectations or results you considered and hoped for before embarking on that project or buying those items you bought yesterday. That gift you gave to that friend, the kindness you showed that family or that colleague; what were the reasons behind those charities? What are you going to do with that car and the clothes you bought, that money or savings in your account?

From the above definition one may now ask, "What was I made to do here or why do I exist? What was God's intention for creating me or bringing me into this life?"

The Bible is clear that God created us for His own glory (Isaiah 43:7) and pleasure (Revelation 4:11). He made us all differently so that we can do different things in life, while pursuing that purpose. Like a body having diverse parts so are we as a church. Each part is expected to function according to its endowments; the hands doing what they are meant to do, the eyes, the nose, the mouth, even the legs, intestines, gonads and others are to do the same. As a body none is expected to work in isolation from the other. There should be harmony in operations for the primary purpose of having a healthy, vibrant and productive body that will reverence and give God glory. Every other thing we do should reflect that. King Solomon underscored that and by the Spirit of God said,

"Let us hear the conclusion of the whole matter: Fear God, and keep his commandments: for this is the whole duty of man. For God shall bring every work into judgment, with every secret thing, whether it be good, or whether it be evil." Ecclesiastics 12:13-14 KJV

From the above passage you will see that whatever we do in this life will pass through the yardstick of, ***"Fear God and keep His commandments,"*** or simply put: love for God. Also, it is not just enough to be doing something "good", but for what purpose? Is it for self-promotion or love for God? When it passes through God's scrutiny, would it have met His standards? That should be the billion dollar question; that should also be our aim. This is Apostle Paul's take on this.

"My conscience is clear, but that does not make me innocent. It is the Lord who judges me. Therefore, judge nothing before the appointed time; wait until the Lord comes. He will bring to light what is hidden

in darkness and will expose the motives of the heart. At that time each will receive their praise from God." 1 Corinthians 4:4-5 NIV

Jesus corroborated the same thing with King Solomon by saying, ***"Love God with all your heart, with all your soul, with all your mind and your neighbor as yourself" (Mark 12:30-31).*** Everything we do should fall in line with this assertion. This should be what dictates whatever activities – vocation and trade or other things – we find ourselves in because they are part of our duties in fulfilling our purpose. Whether you are a business executive, a pastor, inventor or a politician, His purpose for making you should be the driving factor as you undertake these endeavors. You are an extension of God in those areas you operate. In those areas He equipped you with various talents, you are there to represent Him, to serve Him and be a blessing to His people and humanity.

Your gifts define your Assignment.

"And God blessed them, and God said unto them, 'Be fruitful, and multiply, and replenish the earth, and subdue it: and have dominion over the fish of the sea, and over the fowl of the air, and over every living thing that moveth upon the earth'." Genesis 1:28 KJV

Get d' picture!

Whatever gifts God gave us was to enable us as a people to run and prosper the Earth. He wants us to run it as a prudent gardener would run a farm. But instead of being fruitful and encouraging fruitfulness as He commanded, many are doing otherwise. Today, there are high killings and mass murder, abortions, anti-people policies among others due to greed and self. There is hatred being spread across board. There is war both visible and invisible. How does it concern me, Dennis, you may ask? How it concerns you is that you can play certain roles to influence things here. There are certain things you alone can handle and make a change but another would find hard to fit in there. Your duty here is to locate those and engage them. This could be in any form you are at home with, but channeled towards reaching the hurting and emotionally wounded; letting them have first-hand experience of God's love through you. If it is teaching, teach the truth; if it is encouraging others show empathy as you encourage them; if it is helping in any way, help cheerfully. Find out whatever you are good at that can be of benefit, use it to bless someone. Let there be that urgency and attraction in working to see that God's will is done in this place.

Some people were privileged to have had their cake cut out for them; their roles in pursuing their purpose were handed down to them instead of them digging to find out what they were made to do in this life. As a result, they never wasted a lot of time trying to determine that, rather they went full force pursuing them. We know people like Joseph, Samuel and David. As a Bible student you will remember that it was that revelation that earned Joseph envy and hatred from his siblings. Prophet Samuel, right from his childhood was sent to serve

God in the temple. David's own purpose brought him at a crossroad with King Saul.

However, there are those that have to sit down, seek to find out their roles in fulfilling their purpose – Why was I made?

If I may ask, "What are you good at?" Can you be precise in answering that question? Which one do you love doing the most, the one that gives you utmost satisfaction when you do it? What do friends and those that know you closely say you are very good at?

Now let us do some personal analysis. Get a pen and paper, go into your room and stay quiet. Possibly, lock your door and do not allow any distractions.

Think through and write down ten things you feel you are good at. Note those ones you love doing the most and those that give you maximum satisfaction when you do them. When you have finished with that, look for your sincere friends. On a serious note ask these friends what they think you can do best; check them out on that list. Listen to their comments, find out why they think you can do what and analyze them. Also ask your family members the same questions, especially Mom and Dad. Check all these things out too. Now, go back to that list, look at them closely, which of them scored the highest mark? Do you think you can handle that? Do you think you have the resources or can garner enough resources to pursue that? Do you derive joy doing that? Check the next in line with high marks and the third do the same thing

Get d' picture!

too. Out of the top three you may choose one you have the variables to achieve with utmost ease. I hope this helps you.

Remember also that all of us are endowed differently. Some are technically inclined, many artistically inclined, others academically inclined. Many have more than one endowment combined, depending on their strength but the most important thing is the way we approach our talents. How we develop and run with them matters a lot. That also determines how we succeed at the end and how God would eventually use us.

"And the LORD spake unto Moses, saying, 'See, I have called by name Bezaleel the son of Uri, the son of Hur, of the tribe of Judah: And I have filled him with the spirit of God, in wisdom, and in understanding, and in knowledge, and in all manner of workmanship, To devise cunning works, to work in gold, and in silver, and in brass, And in cutting of stones, to set them, and in carving of timber, to work in all manner of workmanship. And I, behold, I have given with him Aholiab, the son of Ahisamach, of the tribe of Dan: and in the hearts of all that are wise hearted I have put wisdom, that they may make all that I have commanded thee'." Exodus 31:1-6 KJV

When you look at the above passage, you will discover that you are not an accident as some would like to claim or think, and want us to believe. No, nothing is here by accident or just for the sake of being here. Those gifts and skills in you are not there by chance. Someone put them in you. All the gadgets and appliances in a GM car were installed there by a GM engineer. The car itself was also built by an engineer for a reason. A house is built by someone for shelter and protection, same with a car for easy, comfortable and fast movement. God that created you made you for a purpose. Even trash bags are made for something. There is something God has put in you to distinguish you from me and make you a blessing to me and others. Discover that, develop it and improve on it. The money you are looking for may be tied to that gift or talent. If all of us have the same gifts and talents, then we may not be useful to one another after all. So, run and stop the time wasting. Find out what your role is in fulfilling that purpose and stay with it.

A little digression here please: someone is behind every intelligent design. Note also that even "unintelligent" designs were also made by someone. That something does not make sense to you does not mean that it makes no sense to the maker. The perfect working of human body is a clear indication of intelligent design, likewise the rotation and revolution of the earth. All of them point to intelligent design, and they each were made for a particular purpose. Rotation deals with day and night issues while revolution deals with seasons.

You are in God's agenda made to serve His purpose. Your duty is to discover your role and pursue it. God, the master creator and strategist, also allows everything that comes your way in life to shape and prepare you for that assignment. The experience may not be what you want but at the end you discover why it was necessary. You are not a spectator who does not participate in the actions of a game, neither are you a Dead Sea that only receives but not give out. You are a

Get d' picture!

participant and a player here, unlike the Dead Sea you are made to flow out and nourish your environment and community.

There are other ways of determining your role in fulfilling your purpose in life.

Some say that whatever you have a comparative advantage in doing is most likely your role in fulfilling that purpose. Others are of the view that whatever you do with utmost ease and joy is what you were made to do. Another school of thought says it is those things that give you concern or irritate you that you are made to take care of. There is this group that says whatever you are passionate about is most likely your role in accomplishing your purpose.

When you analyze the above statements, you will discover there are truths in all of them. You may be thinking, Dennis, what do you mean? In economics for instance, it is what a country or company has a comparative advantage in producing that it focuses its energy and resources on. If producing cars would be cheaper and more rewarding than producing diesel trucks, it becomes in the interest of the company to invest more in producing cars. You cannot be a Jack of all trades while mastering none. You can be virtually talented in many areas but you should be known for being an expert in something (a field). Every one of us can do one thing or the other but there is that area you knock everyone else out with just a wink. That could be an area you need to look into. This is the area you will put in a little energy and come out with tremendous results.

Concerning those that advocate that fulfilling your purpose could be linked to dealing with those things that irritate or are of concern to you, I also agree with them in that I have heard that some people that joined the armed forces to fight overseas did that out of concerns that if the bad guys were not stopped over there they could import their evil and murderous acts to our homeland. This is also what I heard about some officers who joined the police. They detest crime; as a result, they joined the police to help fight it. Some people that survived certain conditions and diseases have become strong advocates against such. Some have even gone further to promote research and legislations against them.

For those that say that fulfilling your purpose could be linked to your passion, I cannot agree more. Passion is a strong motivator. It is what gives you resilience. I have seen people passionate about cooking; I have seen others passionate about sharing the gospel. I have seen people passionate about helping the needy and many more. Some are passionate about children. I do not know but I think everyone is passionate about something. I mean something good, something uplifting, something godly. Anything you are passionate about, you discover you find yourself doing without much stress, you are happy doing it but to an onlooker it may look hard. I know a lot of folks that hate teaching; I also know a lot of passionate teachers. When you pursue your passion you touch and change lives and at the long run it can give you money and wealth.

Any of the above could be indicative of the role God wants you to play in fulfilling your purpose here on earth.

Get d' picture!

The Bible says that the gift of a man is what makes a room for him and brings him before great men (Proverbs 18:16). Your assignment is in your gift. What are you gifted on? Gifts serve some purpose. A good singer and worshipper will bring down the glory of God. The individual can also be refreshing to hurting souls. If you are a good salesman or a persuasive speaker, you could make a good preacher or politician. You can also be a good lawyer. These are powerful gifts. Once you discover your gifts, they will help you to find your assignments and also aid you to do them. It is someone's gifts or abilities that oftentimes determine what they become and also their reach in life. In Ephesians 4:8-12, the Bible also says that he that descended is he that arose and gave gift to all men for the purpose of building the church. All these talents, all these abilities and gifts were from God to enable us be what we are made to be, improve our lots as a body of Christ and be a blessing to our communities. Now, our duty is to discover and focus on that which we are privileged to have received and improve on them.

The Bible commands us to be diligent. So, whatever your hands find doing, do it with all diligence (Ecclesiastics 9:10; Colossians 3:23). That may be the avenue to fulfilling your purpose and assignment in life.

1. You are Christ's ambassador

When the States Department sends an envoy to a country, that individual is there to represent the United States, not the host country. The person's preoccupation would be to showcase good aspects of the country, things that abound in his home country and persuade the host and its citizens to take advantage of those resources or services. The end result or purpose of those efforts is to bring benefits to his country. Although he is in that country, he remains a U.S. citizen depending on the protection and provision of the United States. This is the revelation many believers lack today. They live as if they are citizens and at the mercy of this world. No wonder the problems and tragedies of the world befall them. Can you imagine America abandoning its envoy if war, disease or hardship breaks out in his host country? Believers have failed to exercise their rights as citizens of heaven. As a U.S. citizen, if anything happened to the envoy American people would ask questions. This is the same thing for you, child of God. Heaven will query any authority if anything happens to you. The envoy works hard to recruit support for his home country, even making the host to admire the life, goods and services that abound in his home country. He mobilizes people, funds and various interests that would benefit his home country. At the end of his tenure he is re-called back home, after giving the full account of his stewardship he would be rewarded. That is how it is with every believer in Christ. The Bible describes you as Christ's Ambassador (2 Corinthians 5:20), pilgrim (1 Peter 2:11). So your duty is to project God's kingdom here on earth for people to develop interest in the things of God and heaven. Remember, you are here for a limited time.

2. You are a soldier of Christ.

Like I said above, the soldier's duty is to help protect the territorial integrity of his nation and maintain the freedom his people enjoy. A soldier is also equally ready to pay the supreme price to protect his country. Think about this. As a believer, are you sure you are ready to do this for your faith in Christ and the kingdom or would you chicken out and deny the faith when threatened? May God help us here. Many are denying the faith to save their lives, to have a roof over their head and food on their table. The church needs to pray for the persecuted and the oppressed for courage to stand firm in their faith at such trying times. Some of us are seeing the things that are happening in the Middle East and some socialist worlds. It is a call to duty and do not be left out.

3. You are the light and salt of the world.

Light reveals, and helps you see what to do and where to go, how to step and more. As believers we are here to reveal the mind of God to the world to enable them see how to live in the world filled with darkness and evil. Believers are to teach and show the world how to live, love and care. We are also to teach and show them how to be responsible, obey God and take care of our environment.

Salt is a seasoning as well as a preservative. As salt helps make our food well-seasoned and palatable so are believers to make the world we live in livable. Think for a moment about a world where the love of

God or His people is lacking. It will be a horrendous place, chaotic and unlivable.

Before the advent of refrigerators, salt was one of preservatives used in keeping raw flesh from decaying. As a preservative, believers continuing stay on Earth is what is keeping it to date. Once the Holy Spirit leaves and the Church is raptured, God's wrath would be poured and unleashed on this earth to destroy it as the scriptures say. That would usher in then the new heaven and new earth as prophesied by John the revelator (Revelations 21:1).

Knowing that this would be the case we need to double our efforts in pointing many to the cross – the place of their salvation. As they begin to see the love of God through us those that have been appointed to salvation would be helped to make it to the saving grace of God that is in Christ Jesus.

4. God's instrument to restoring His kingdom on Earth

"And he said unto them, 'Go ye into all the world, and preach the gospel to every creature. He that believeth and is baptized shall be saved; but he that believeth not shall be damned'." Mark 16:15-16 KJV

What can I do?

You can do many things. Start by impacting the lives of people you meet day-by-day and brightening the corners wherever you are. It may

Get d' picture!

be in your office, at the mall or market place. It could be in the library or school. Talk to colleagues or partners at business breakfasts or seminars. People are hurting and a lot of them are yearning for help deep inside them. Some do not know how to express it. Those that cannot manage it commit suicide. A show of love, care, concern and compassion can go a long way to make a difference. When you see the rate of suicide and murder in your neighborhood, you will understand what I mean. The Bible says the whole world awaits the manifestation of sons of God (Romans 8:19). They are waiting for you. So, take action and God will bless you.

Present the kingdom you represent in good light and widen its appeal to the people around you or your community.

Bring God closer to your people through your lifestyle. Let them see the beauty of Christ manifested through you towards them.

Can I change a thing or make something better?

Of course you can change things and improve on many things discussed above at some point in time for efficiency and better results.

CHAPTER SEVEN

Safety Ships

In addition to discovering yourself and your purpose from the word of God, you need a lot of "ships" in your life to help you understand yourself and achieve your maximum potential. Some of them are – mentorship, friendship, discipleship/apprenticeship, and fellowship.

1. Mentorship

We are in a world where things move so fast; things move in split seconds. It is a world of robots and remotes. Whenever we touch the buttons we receive instant responses, but life is not always like that. Life is slow and still takes its course. Sometimes you are at a loss of what to do next to get to the next level. That is why to succeed we need mentors in our lives as we navigate the threatening waves and tides of life. Mentorship is a kind of relationship whereby a more experienced or more knowledgeable individual helps to guide a less experienced or less knowledgeable individual. The mentor may be older or younger, but should have a certain area of expertise. A mentor is like an experienced sailor who over time has mastered the sea routes including all the hot spots and turns in them.

We know about Moses and Joshua. We also know about Elijah and Elisha. We have Jesus with His disciples too. These are clear examples where mentoring relationships were discussed in the Bible. There are other examples too.

There may be something you want to do but have no idea on how to go about it. Or you may be new in an organization, perhaps as a new hire or intern; you need a mentor, someone who has got an old hand in the area you will be operating. Look for people that have succeeded in that area, tag on and learn from them. Allow them to mentor you in that particular area. Perhaps you are newly married and want to be a successful and good spouse you need someone to guide you especially those that have succeeded in their relationships. There are some bits and turns you do not know about, things that may not show up until a time. An experienced person will help you know them before they occur so you are not taken unawares or you find a way to avoid them entirely.

You may be a new believer and want to live a life of purity and holiness; you need mentors that you can learn from their lives, even from their errors. I remember those days growing up as young believer, one of my mentors warned me against being too free with the opposite sex in an isolated place or during odd times. According to him, if you know a lady (also applicable to men) you cannot resist and say no to her (his) advances when cornered, avoid every opportunity of the two of you ever being alone in a secluded place. Such place could be dangerous to your faith (purity). That advice was well taken, and it has been useful.

When I was growing up, I loved to see successful Born Again businessmen. Every successful businessman does not really tickle me, but when I see believers among them I get excited. There was this impression that believers were "never do wells." I also know that unbelievers can do anything – ethical or not to be rich. So whenever I see one believer successful I get interested and close to the person. As much as I wanted to be successful I wanted it God's way. My getting close was to know the secrets of his success even as a believer. If you go to developing countries you will understand what I mean, you will discover that businesses are riddled with heavy corruption: manipulations and kickbacks. It is under this type of situation that you need mentorship. There are people of the same faith, God fearing people who God has helped to break the barriers you are afraid of. A connection with them will help you find your way through the shark-infested waters of business in those areas.

2. Friendship

"A friend is someone who knows all about you and still loves you." – Elbert Hubbard. Your friends will help you maximize your potentials and fulfill your purpose. Friends are like mirrors that reflect and help you see what you cannot see on your own if they were not there. What other people would not be bold to tell you, your friends will. The reason is that they do not want to see you fail but to see the best of you. They are also quick to tell you what you can easily achieve and also help you achieve that.

When I was growing up, there was something I learned from my mother about friendship. Those days as we did our house chores, my mother would give each of us the portion that was commensurate to our abilities; she would be watching some of our friends that came to visit with us. Some of the friends will come and help you out so that you can finish on time and go to play with them. Others would just be there looking as you do your chores. At the end of the day mom would say, "You see those people that helped you do your chores, they are truly your friends. If anything happens to you tomorrow they will come and help you. But you see those people that were watching you do your chores alone, they are not your true friends. They will never help you if anything happens to you tomorrow (in the future). As these ones have supported you, when you see them in need support them too. They are your true friends." This was like throwing her weight behind the saying, "A friend in need is a friend indeed."

We also know the story of David and Jonathan. Even though Jonathan knew that David was a threat to his ascending the throne, he still loved him and treated him as his own. He gave David every support he needed and protected him to the best of his ability from his father. When he died David reciprocated that friendship when he was in the position to do so (2 Samuel 9:7).

"And David said unto him, 'Fear not: for I will surely shew thee kindness for Jonathan thy father's sake, and will restore thee all the land of Saul thy father; and thou shalt eat bread at my table continually'." KJV

The value of friendship cannot be overstated. Proverbs 17:17a says that a friend loves at all times; when it is good or when it is bad, when it is convenient and when it is not. It also says in chapter 18:24 that some friends stick closer than a brother. To be successful in your life journey, you need friendship to sail safely to your harbor. You cannot name any successful person that will not tell you their story about their friends. My father and his friend were like twin brothers. They did virtually everything together. They were both in the force and looked out for each other. You need one as you navigate life. Treat them well and respect them. You need to understand that to be treated friendly you also need to show yourself friendly.

3. Discipleship/Apprenticeship

This is the act of subjecting yourself to learn under an experienced hand, a skill. If you have a goal of reaching a certain height in life you will need to look for people that have reached such heights before you. Learn from them how they were able to make it to where they are, their challenges and how they were able to beat them – find out the nitty gritty or bolts and nuts of the entire process. If you cannot reach them look for their works and read their books.

Reading about car repairs is beautiful but actually staying under an experienced mechanic for a period of time for hands on work on faulty or damaged cars is another thing altogether.

Jesus to accomplish His mission on earth – mankind redemption, raised twelve apostles who for three years learned under His feet. They were to take over and continue the Earthly ministry when He returns to heaven. To really understand the mission, He gave them a three-year intensive training. They were with Him morning afternoon and night. They learned the way He talked, prayed, His values and beliefs. At ceremonies and occasions they were with Him. You remember the miracles at Cana of Galilee (John 2:3-9), four and five thousand feeds (Luke 9:10-17). Everything He did and all the places He went they were with Him soaking up all He was teaching and imparting into them.

You saw the outcome when He eventually departed. The gospel and salvation message continued and spread like wild fire. They also did it with boldness accompanied by signs and wonders. If you look closely at all they did, you will discover they just did what the master taught them, and with confidence. You remember the Sanhedrin testified that though they were unlearned but were bold (Acts 4:13). The truth was that their mentor and teacher did a very good job letting them have firsthand experience on the job. A person gains confidence by continuous practice.

When you discover your purpose, going for training will help you develop and improve your capacity to deliver. You also gain a confidence and expertise that you can only have by practice under a seasoned practitioner. His approval of your work is like a seal.

As an apprentice you are under the cover and protection of your teacher or mentor. You are operating on his own account (faith, confidence and expertise) until you develop your own account. As a learner, if you mess things up, your teacher or coach bears the responsibility. That is why it is easy to grow under a coach. I have seen some apprentice mechanics or interns spoil things while working on vehicles, it is the master or teacher that eventually pays to replace the damaged item. But if the damage was done by a regular paid worker, the costs of the replaced part would be deducted from the worker's paycheck.

This is one of the reasons you need the apprenticeship experience to succeed in your chosen career or vocation. You find that as an apprentice you are under your master's cover as you practice. With that you are exposed to learn more. The heat does not reach you directly until you gain professional independence and become an expert.

4. Fellowship

Another ship you may need to sail safely to your harbor is fellowship. It is a friendly association, mainly with people that share common interests. In our churches we have fellowships, in our professions we have fellowships and also social activities we have fellowships. But one thing is clear about them, they all are pursuing what is to better the lots and enhance the welfare of members.

Fellowships at times organize seminars, conferences and trainings for members on things that can improve their capacities and usefulness in their career and life.

They also provide support and help where applicable. Remember the Bible enjoins us not to neglect the coming together of believers as some do (Hebrews 10:25), showing you the importance of fellowship.

CHAPTER EIGHT

People that had a glimpse of who they were

In this place we want to take a look at folks that had a glimpse of who they were and what they did when faced with daunting life challenges.

Before Adam fell, he had dominion over the Earth. Everything was subject to him. The Bible recorded that he even gave names to everything that God made and brought before him (Genesis 2:19-20). That was indeed a great feat. He was fully in charge of things around him. But once he failed, he lost that dominion and the God nature in him, and degenerated to become just an ordinary human. I believe he was made to live forever and be in charge of this estate – the Earth, but the fall changed everything and man began to die. Nature and all it contains began to rebel against him.

However, along the line there have been godly men who have at one point or the other dared to reestablish that dominion, which Adam lost. We are going to look at some of them and their stories even though they have been told countless times.

Joseph

At about 17, Joseph caught the vision God had for him in life. With that he set out to accomplishing it and shared same to his siblings but that disclosure marked the beginning of a grand conspiracy against him. But God, whom he trusted and respected so much, would not let him down or be derailed. He was sold into slavery. At that place he was set up by the wife of his boss and was jailed because of his integrity. But that did not stop him, he never sulked, Joseph continued to look forward, believing that one day the God of his parents would deliver him and bring him to his place of destiny. Eventually He did deliver him, not only that he was delivered, God elevated him also above his captors. He became a Prime Minister and was instrumental to saving Egypt and the entire region from famine, thereby fulfilling God's vision for his life. I do not know about your situation now. You may be suffering injustice; perhaps there was a conspiracy against you to bring you down at all cost. My advice to you is that God is watching, remain faithful to Him. He will deliver at the appropriate time. He would shame your enemies. Anything you think you are missing right now He would restore. So do not be downcast or resort to doubt and to cast aspersions on God. That is what the tempter would want, to damage

Get d' picture!

your relationship and testimony before God. Do not yield to that, your time is coming. Take a cue from Joseph.

Moses

Moses, despite being raised in the palace as an Egyptian prince, preferred to identify with his people – the Jews. As a result, he ran foul to an unwritten code of not dealing with "that kind of people." To add salt to injury, he killed an Egyptian slave master maltreating a Jew. When he discovered that his act has become an open secret, he fled knowing that the royalty would come after him sooner than imagined.

It was at the place of his exile that he had an encounter with God and his life changed forever. God revealed Himself to him and used him to deliver His people from the hand of the Pharaoh and the Egyptians. If you read the book of Exodus in the Bible you will get the whole story. Remember that at a time during the mission, God told him He has made him a god to Pharaoh (Exodus 7:1). Moses never disappointed but unleashed the power of God on that land and their oppressors were forced to let them go. That you have not started seeing the hand of God over your circumstances does not mean that God does not know you are there or has forgotten you. No, if that is your thought, discard it. God is arranging appropriate tools to get you out of your difficulties. As He did for the people of Israel so also will He do for you. He is no respecter of persons nor is there any shadow of turning with Him, whatever He has done for one He will do for the other.

Joshua

After the death of Moses, God commissioned Joshua to lead His people to the Promised Land. He promised to be with him as He was with Moses. As Joshua obeyed, God used him to do many mighty miracles as they marched all the way to the Land. You heard about the falling of the Jericho wall (Joshua 6:20), stilling the sun to enable them fully defeat their enemy (Joshua 10:12-14) and crossing over the Jordan River (Joshua 3). These were some of the things God used Joshua to do as he obeyed and walked with Him. If you can make yourself available, God can also use you to do greater things. He has not changed. He remains faithful.

Caleb

Caleb was one of the spies sent to search out Jericho before its invasion. He was among the small group that brought back good report to Moses even though their report was not believed by the people. But that position endeared him to God. It was only him and Joshua among the twelve spies sent out that entered the Promised Land, the only two that believed that God was able to give them the land they went to spy out. Eventually they were rewarded for their faith and position in God.

What do you see when things seem hard; opportunity or problems? This determines how far and successful you become in life. So many people usually see wolves but few see meat, food, fun out of

Get d' picture!

that animal. Think about it. What is staring at you right now may be the opportunity you have been praying for all years but you are only seeing a problem. Are you laid off a job? Good! That means you need a job change, a new status. It is not a problem, it is an opportunity. Dennis, what are you saying, you may ask? What I am saying is that this is a time to engage your brain and think outside the box. It is a time and an opportunity to learn a skill, trade or any vocation and own your own business and start hiring people instead of you looking for who will hire you. You become a boss, job giver instead of job receiver or job seeker when you create a business. With that you know what? No one fires you again. Learn to see opportunities where others only see problems. That is the difference between successful and unsuccessful people.

Samson

Samson was a destiny child who was born to judge the people of Israel. Like Jesus, his birth was foretold by an angel (Judges 13:2-3). If you read his story you will understand he was a special breed, a Nazarene (Judges 13:4-5). But along the way, due to his flesh and lusts he missed it. Eventually he paid dearly for it (Judges 16:20-21). But when he remembered the Lord he called upon Him and he avenged his enemies (Judges 16:27-30).

Deborah

She was an influential prophetess that judged Israel during her time. God used her to deliver the people from the hands of the Canaanites (Judges 4). She was not afraid of going to war when the man appointed by God to execute the war was afraid of doing that. She provided him the needed support and they got the victory.

Jephthah

Although he came from a not so impressive background, Jephthah was used by God to deliver His people at a time of need. His mother was a harlot; his father's household rejected him as a member of the family. But God did not reject him, rather chose him to deliver His people. It was a time when Israel was being drawn into a war by the Ammonites, descendants of Lot (Judges 11). Jephthah led the people, they routed the Ammonites and God gave them victory and Israel was restored.

You may be thinking or looking at yourself like Jephthah, perhaps due to your background that you cannot amount to anything. You do not see a way over that challenge, over that difficulty. The devil may be telling you you are a disgrace due to one or two things you did wrong. Perhaps it may be because of something that happened that you do not even have control over that the devil is telling you one story or

Get d' picture!

the other. Rebuke the devil! Resist him. The Bible wants you to know this:

"Who shall lay anything to the charge of God's elect? It is God that justifieth. Who is he that condemneth? It is Christ that died, yea rather, that is risen again, who is even at the right hand of God, who also maketh intercession for us." Romans 8:33-34 KJV

So do not allow anything or anyone to hoodwink you. When God justifies you, no one can condemn you, not even yourself can do that. So cheer up and belt up. You are a child of God. God has justified you, when you gave your life to Jesus Christ. It is time to take the fight to the enemy's camp. It is time to go out, obtain the victory and be who we are made to be. What God did through Jephthah He can replicate through you over that circumstance. See yourself as He is seeing you. The Bible says, as He is, so are we in this life.

"Herein is our love made perfect, that we may have boldness in the day of judgment: because as he is, so are we in this world." 1 John 4:17 KJV

Whatever Christ is, that is what you are, so start acting and seeing yourself that way.

Elijah

At a time when the people of God were groping in darkness, Elijah showed up and redirected them back to God. He challenged the powers that be at the time at his own peril but God kept him safe. When the time was ripe, God Himself showed up to prove to the people that He was still the true God that has always been with them.

At this time was when Jezebel held sway in the land crushing anything that stood on her way. Being the queen in Israel she used her position of influence and imported Baal prophets and worship into the land. She saw to it that the worship of the true God was disrupted but made Baal worship instead the official state worship, thereby defiling the land. It could be likened to today when the worship of God has been prohibited in our public places. Any other practice can take place in public domain but not the worship of the true God. If someone prays in the name of Jesus in a school or public function he is hounded and nearly taken or seen as a felon.

It was at this time that Elijah showed up. With godly fury he locked up heaven and there was no rain in the entire kingdom for three and a half years to register God's displeasure over ungodly practices in the land. It was a protest against the king and his misrule. I do not know if we still have men of such character and boldness in church leadership today. If you look at the book of James, the apostle described him as a man of like passion (James 5). This means that there was nothing spectacular about this man only that he knew God and also followed Him passionately.

"Elias was a man subject to like passions as we are, and he prayed earnestly that it might not rain: and it rained not on the earth by the space of three years and six months. And he prayed again, and the

Get d' picture!
heaven gave rain, and the earth brought forth her fruit." James 5:17-18 KJV

Elijah was able to do this because he understood who he was and God's purpose for his life. You remember that at the peak of the drought when he met with Ahab, the king; the king called him the "troubler of Israel" but he would not take it, instead he told the king to his face that the king and his household were the ones troubling Israel.

"And it came to pass, when Ahab saw Elijah, that Ahab said unto him, Art thou he that troubleth Israel? And he (Elijah) answered, I have not troubled Israel; but thou, and thy father's house, in that ye have forsaken the commandments of the LORD, and thou hast followed Baalim." 1 Kings 18:17-18 KJV

When the stage was set, the prophet gathered the people and said, "Today is a day of decision! You either choose to worship the true God or Baal; let the god that answers by fire be god indeed!" With that, the exhibitions by the differing parties involved and the miracles that God let happen that day Elijah restored the worship of the true God to the land. You can too child of God. God is only waiting for you to act and He would perfect every other thing.

Elisha

I see Elisha as the Jesus (literally) of the Old Testament in that he did virtually all the miracles Jesus did in the New Testament. He had

His kind of audacity and authority. Unlike his master Elijah, he was bold and spoke to the powers that be to their face without retreat. You remember the way he addressed the king's commander that was sent to kill him as a result of the devastating famine in the land.

"Then Elisha said, 'Hear ye the word of the LORD; Thus saith the LORD, To morrow about this time shall a measure of fine flour be sold for a shekel, and two measures of barley for a shekel, in the gate of Samaria.' Then a lord on whose hand the king leaned answered the man of God, and said, 'Behold, if the LORD would make windows in heaven, might this thing be?' And he said, 'Behold, thou shalt see it with thine eyes, but shalt not eat thereof'." 2 Kings 7:1-2 KJV

Unlike Elijah that ran away from Jezebel, Elisha sat down in the house and readied to confront the king's messenger.

"But Elisha sat in his house, and the elders sat with him; and the king sent a man from before him: but ere the messenger came to him, he said to the elders, 'See ye how this son of a murderer hath sent to take away mine head? Look, when the messenger cometh, shut the door, and hold him fast at the door: is not the sound of his master's feet behind him'?" 2 Kings 6:32 KJV

He could do that because he understood who he was and who was backing him. You should be the next in line doing the same thing, exercising the power of God, bringing glory and honor to our father, the most High God.

Get d' picture!
David

David was a man that discovered God in various forms. You see this from his writings and songs. He lived a life of total dependency on God both as an individual, as a shepherd, as a soldier and as a king. The books of 1st and 2nd Samuel, books of Psalms, 1st Chronicles among others attest to this. Personally his life and humility have had a great influence in me. He was so selfless. He was also human, a man with many shortcomings but at the same time exceptional. Writing about him will take a lifetime to complete.

John

John the revelator was the beloved of the Lord Himself while on His earthly ministry. He followed Jesus closely at almost every point of His ministry. He witnessed the teachings, miracles, the killing and the resurrection of the Lord. Eventually during the persecution and killing of the followers of Jesus he was imprisoned in the Island of Patmos. There Jesus revealed to him all that is contained in the book of revelation about the end of time.

Kenneth Hagin

Doctors told him he would not be seeing his seventeenth birthday, but he died at the age of 86 a fulfilled man of God. Growing up, tests showed he had a deformed heart and an incurable blood disease. At age 15 he became bedfast but his grandmother would not let go. It was at this time that he encountered Jesus and the healing power of God. God turned around his situation and gave him the mandate to teach His people faith. Today, many see him as the father of the modern faith movement.

CONCLUSION

Reading this book is evidence that God loves you. This book is another testament of God's acts among men. He has not ceased attending to issues of concern to humanity. Also, He has not ceased to be interested in you and all that concern you as an individual. So, as you read, take a moment and ask yourself in sincerity, "Have I really made peace with this good God?"

If you are not born again and reading this book, perhaps you are having series of challenges but will like to have a permanent freedom and succeed in life. First, you need the Lord Jesus Christ in your life today. Stop running your life yourself before you wreck it. Jesus can take you through life in victory. The Bible says that those that are born of God overcome the world.

"For whatsoever is born of God overcometh the world: and this is the victory that overcometh the world, even our faith." 1 John 5:4 (KJV)

We are born again when we realize we are helpless sinners bound for hell without Christ, and when we voluntarily invite and receive Him into our lives as Lord and Savior, after confessing and renouncing our sins.

"But as many as receive Him, to them gave He the power to become sons of God, even to them that believe on His name." John 1:12 (KJV)

If this is your choice, take this prayer with me after confessing your sins before God.

"Lord Jesus, come into my life, be the Lord of my life. I accept you today as my Lord and Savior. Thank you because I am born again. Amen."

Congratulations my friend! God bless you. You are welcomed into the family of God today. You need to begin a walk and relationship with God. First, locate a Bible believing and Holy Ghost filled church and fellowship group in your locality. Once that is done, join with your new found Christian brothers and sisters and begin to fellowship with them. You should also make sure to attend the mid-week and weekly programs of your new Church family.

For questions and other inquiries please email: kandjventures04@gmail.com

Get d' picture!

Again, God bless you. Know this; life is not complete without Christ – Shalom!

ABOUT THE AUTHOR

Dennis Kenechukwu is an Evangelist, speaker and teacher. He is also an author and writer. He promotes the gospel of the Lord Jesus Christ and carries it to the lost world. His message of hope, change and dominion is to empower the church to retake its rightful position and enjoy the benefits thereof as heirs of the kingdom. It is also to motivate her to fully embrace the Great Commission, which was handed over to her before the Lord Jesus ascended back to heaven.

At Enugu, Dennis served as a Youth Pastor and member of the Sunday School Board in his local church. There also he taught Sunday School for many years.

He helped plant churches in many Nigerian cities of Lokoja, Warri and Port Harcourt. He has also preached the good news of the gospel to many cultures and peoples.

Dennis also worked as a news reporter for the English – to – Africa Service of the Voice of America for many years.

www.ingramcontent.com/pod-product-compliance
Lightning Source LLC
Chambersburg PA
CBHW071310060426
42444CB00034B/1765